SUFI SAINTS
of
East & West

SUFI SAINTS
of
East & West

Sadhu T. L. Vaswani

Edited with an Introduction by
J. P. Vaswani

STERLING PUBLISHERS PRIVATE LIMITED

STERLING PUBLISHERS PRIVATE LIMITED
A-59, Okhla Industrial Area, Phase-II, New Delhi-110020
Tel: 6916209, 6916165, 6912677, 6910050 Fax: 6331241
E-mail: ghai@nde.vsnl.net.in; www.sterlingpublishers.com

Sufi Saints of East & West
© 2002, Sadhu T. L. Vaswani
ISBN 81 207 2360 0

All rights are reserved. No part of this publication may be reproduced, stored in a retrieval system or transmitted, in any form or by any means, mechanical, photocopying, recording or otherwise, without prior written permission of the original publisher.

PRINTED IN INDIA

Published by Sterling Publishers Pvt. Ltd., New Delhi-110 020.
Lasertypeset at Vikas Compographics, New Delhi-110 020.
Printed at Sai Printers, New Delhi-110 020.

CONTENTS

Introduction 7

Friends of God 16

Rabia: Mira of Islam 32

Abu Hasan 59

Junnuna Misri 84

Sachal Sarmast 100

Yusuf, the Beautiful 117

Parasi: A Muslim Yogi 130

Hatim Hashim 139

Ahmed: A Lover of Allah 146

INTRODUCTION

Who is a friend of God?

He who has seen the Face of God unveiled, has spoken to Him, and has a direct knowledge of Him. He lives and moves and dedicates all he is and all he has to God. Such a one, in the words of an ancient book, possesses nothing and is God-possessed. Love of God is the one only treasure of his life. The friend of God lives, from day to day, in the intoxication of love.

In the following pages have been brought together, sketches of Sufi mystics–Friends and Lovers of God–written by Sadhu Vaswani, at different times. All of them were men and women of communion and compassion. They rejoiced in God as the One Beloved of the Heart. For them, to live was to love God and His suffering children. And love, in the words of a Sufi mystic, is "a fire in the Heart consuming all, save the will of the Beloved".

"Our wills are ours that we may make them Thine!" said a Christian mystic. And the Sufi mystics, concerning whom Sadhu Vaswani speaks to us, renounced self-will as they walked the way of love. It was a Sufi Saint who sang:

> If thou wouldst tread
> The Path of Love
> Thou must first become
> Humble as ashes and dust!
> Be as dust on His Path!

The pilgrim on the Path of Love must reduce himself to naught, be nothing, no-thing. And to be no-thing is to become new, is to be re-born. The way to God is the way to re-birth. We are born of the flesh: we have to be born of the Spirit. Hence the need of purification, purgation. "Freed from passion must thou be", said Sadhu Vaswani, "and become a temple of the Holy Spirit". Therefore must we submit ourselves to a process of purgation—as by fire. Passing through the fire we, too, may shine one day, like molten gold, in the beauty of the One Beloved.

What is the meaning of the word "sufi"? According to some, it is derived from the Arabic word "suf", which means "wool". The earliest Sufis were ascetics who wore coarse garments of wool, a symbol of voluntary poverty and renunciation of the world and its pleasures.

There are some who associate the word "sufi" with the word "safa", which means "pure". The great Sufi poet and saint, Jalal ud-Din Rumi, when asked, "What makes the Sufi"? answered, "Purity of the heart, not the patched mantle!" The true Sufi is a man of purity, inner purity of the heart. He rejoices in a life of poverty and prayer, of simplicity, sympathy and sacrifice. He accepts suffering and pain as gifts from God and grows in purity, from more to more. For, without purification, there is no illumination: and without illumination, there is no unification, the goal of the Sufi's quest.

According to some, the word "sufi" is linked with "ahl al-suffa", which means "the people of the bench". They were the men, who, in the days of the Prophet Muhammad, sat by day and slept by night, on the benches outside the mosque where the Prophet worshipped. They kept away from the world. They were men of non-possession. They ate what was given to them and wore simple, coarse garments.

There are some again who associate the word "sufi" with the Greek word "sophia", which means "wisdom". The true

Sufi is a seeker of wisdom. In his life mingle the two streams of love and wisdom.

The faith of the Sufi rises above all creeds and all denominations and religions. It is a way of life–the life of faith and freedom and love. It seeks to set men free from the bondage of creeds and dogmas, of rites and ceremonies, calling them away from all things extern to the interior life of the Spirit. The Sufi emphasis is on inner experience and ecstasy, rather than on deductive reasoning or positive tradition. It is the way of the Heart – the Heart which turns, at all times and in all conditions, to the One Only Beloved.

Sadhu Vaswani was always at home when he spoke or wrote concerning the great Sufi mystics. It was as though he was one of them. His own life was one of detachment and dedication, of self-denial, service and silent sacrifice.

"Who are you?" Sadhu Vaswani was asked, one day. And he answered, "I am a Sufi! I worship Beauty, and Love is my sacrament of life. I adore the Lord as Blessed Beauty, as Immortal Love. Wheresover Love appears, I bend in reverent worship. For there shines the very Light of God!"

Love is the magic key, which opens the door of every heart. And with love and deep understanding, Sadhu Vaswani writes concerning the Sufi mystics, whose sketches are given in the following pages. Little wonder, his words are clear and simple, charged with a strange, mystic power; they are uniquely alive.

The goal of life, according to the Sufi mystics, is union with God. And the very first step is repentance (*tauba*), or conversion. True conversion is a change of mind and heart. It is a gift of grace. When God or a God-man looks upon someone in grace, the soul within him is awakened. And he realises that the years spent in accumulating the wealth or honours of the earth were wasted in vain. Life is too short and no further time must be wasted in pursuing the vanities of the world. The awakened soul turns his back on worldly pleasures and longs for union with the One Beloved. He lives a life of self-control and self-denial, without which no progress may be made on the Path.

Awakening comes in a variety of ways. But it is always a gift of grace. To Ibrahim, the king of Balkh, awakening came through a dream in which he saw some angels of God looking for something on the roof of his palace.

"What are you seeking?" he asked them. And they answered, "We have lost a camel!" In sheer amazement, the king exclaimed, "Is it not foolish, O angels, to search for a camel on the roof of a palace?" Quietly, one of the angels remarked, "Is it not equally foolish, O king, to search for God in the midst of the pleasures of the palace?" The words went deep into the heart of the king and, when he awoke, he resolved to renounce the palace and set out as a *fakir* in quest of God.

Awakening came to Shibli, when he was in the king's court. The king had distributed costly robes among his nobles. One of them, given to fits of sneezing, wiped his nose with the sleeves of his robe. When the matter came to the king's notice, he dismissed the nobleman from the court, saying, "Is this how you make use of the robe I gave you?" The words brought awakening to Shibli's heart. "The King of kings," he said to himself, "has given me the precious robe of the human body: to what use have I put it all these years? If God takes me to account, what answer shall I give?"

With awakening comes the realisation that the body is a Temple of God. It must not be soiled; it must be kept clean and pure, so that it might become a channel of God's forces in this world of darkness and death. In this thought is the seed of true repentance or conversion—the very first step on the Path. And the second step is fear of God. The penitent soul lives in fear, lest he may do something which offends the Lord. Fear has a place in the life of the servant of God. It was Guru Nanak who said, "The heart which loves God, fears Him!" And fear inspires constant watchfulness and vigilance over the heart.

Fear of God leads to detachment—the third stage on the Sufi Path. For the love of God, the soul renounces everything that is non-God. The root of all sin and suffering is attachment to things of the earth. True detachment is inner – it is detachment from desires which stain the purity of the soul. True detachment is nothing extern. Raja Janak, living in the palace, was detached in the heart within. A *sanyasin*, who owned only a loin-cloth, was not free from attachment.

He who lives in the fear of God and longs for union with the Beloved, has no care or worry about money or possessions, pomp or glory, honours or earthly greatness. He breaks the fetters which tie him to earthly things or creatures; he strips himself of everything to follow the Master. Was this not the teaching Jesus gave to the young Prince who had followed the commandments but had not yet entered the Kingdom? To him, said Jesus, "Sell all you have and give to the poor; then come and follow me!" And when a disciple said to him, "Permit me, Master, to go and bury my father," Jesus answered, "Let the dead bury their own dead!"

As the pilgrim treads the Path, he learns to be detached even from his detachment: he is absorbed in the love of God. The world and its pleasures and power no longer attract him. He has attained to freedom.

Then comes the fourth stage, a very important step on the Path. It is poverty, the inner poverty of the Spirit. It does not consist merely of non-possession of worldly wealth or goods, though it includes it. "I have not found the true knowledge of God," said Bayazid, "except in a hungry stomach and a naked body." True poverty, however, is more an emptiness of the heart than of the hand or the stomach. A man may possess all the world and yet be poor. Another may possess nothing and yet not be poor. For true poverty is humility of the heart. It is the knowledge of one's own nothingness. *Naham! Naham! Tuho! Tuho!* – I am nothing, O Lord! Thou alone art!

Poverty, therefore, means utter dependence upon God, not upon the things of the earth. The truly poor man is the lord of the earth. He has cast his cares upon God, and lives free from worry and anxiety. If he is anxious about anything, he has not yet become poor. He will not ask for anything from any man, and will receive whatever comes to him as from the hand of God. He regards worldly wealth as ashes and dust.

True poverty is self-denial, renunciation of "self". The truly poor man has no existence apart from God. He chooses nothing, neither poverty nor affluence. He rejoices in whatever station the Lord places him in. He seeks nothing but God. He desires nothing, he wills nothing. His desire and will are merged in the desire and will of God.

The fifth stage is that of patience. Patience is the alchemist who turns every blow into a blessing, every burden into a benediction. As the pilgrim moves on the Path, he is tried and tested, as gold is tested by being thrown into the crucible. Significant are the words of Hudayfa al-Yaman, "When God loves a servant, He proves him by suffering." If he is patient, he will not avoid suffering, but will greet it with a smile, knowing that all that comes from God is good.

The man of patience thrives on suffering: the more he suffers, the more his soul shines. The great Sufi teacher and mystic, Jalal ud-Din Rumi, unfolds a very beautiful picture in his *Masnavi*. He writes, "There is an animal called the porcupine. It is made stout and big by blows of the stick. The more you cudgel it, the more it thrives. The soul of a true believer is, verily, a porcupine. The more it is chastised, the more it thrives. So it is that God's chosen ones have to bear a greater share of suffering than other worldly men. Suffering gives strength to their souls."

The sixth stage is of *tawakkul* or self-surrender. It is entrusting oneself to God, completely, entirely, utterly. It is passing out of oneself so that nothing of oneself remains – alone, the Beloved exists!

Once Bayazid was asked by an *imam* to assist him at the Friday congregational prayer. At the close of it, the *imam* asked Bayazid, "You do not work for wages and you do not beg for alms: how do you live?" To this Bayazid answered, "Let me offer the prayer again! A prayer recited behind an *imam*, who does not know who gives us our daily bread, cannot be valid."

It was Hatim who said, "It is our business to worship God as He bade us. It is His business to provide us with daily sustenance, as He promised us."

Tawakkul does not mean that a person must do no work. Rightly says the Gita, "To work you have the right, but not to the fruit thereof!" This is the spirit of *tawakkul*. Do your work, do it in the best way you can. But do not be bothered about the results of your work. "Sow the seed, then rely upon the Lord!"

The seventh and the last stage is gratitude. The pilgrim on the Path has now arrived at a stage where he is grateful to God for whatever comes his way. Does he fall sick? He praises the Lord. Has he suffered a loss? He praises the Lord. He feels sure that the Beloved can never mean harm, the Creator's pen can never slip! He is always happy and contented. In his prayers, he will never ask God for a thing to happen or another to be averted. He knows that not a leaf moves, not a straw turns, not a lip stirs, except if it be the will of God. And whatever the Lord wills, is the very best that can ever happen. God's will becomes his own will. Significant are the words of Jami, "The Sufi has no individual will. His will is obliterated in the will of God, nay, indeed, his will is the very will of God." And when this happens, man wants nothing: he lacks nothing. He lives in a state of at-one-ment with God. And as those around him look at him, they exclaim, "We have seen God!"

So lived the Sufi mystics, the "Friends of God", concerning whom Sadhu Vaswani – who himself was a "Friend of God" – has so much to tell us in the following pages. To them, God was the One Only Reality of Life. And they found God in the Heart within. The way by which they walked was the Way of Love. And love, as a great Sufi mystic said, lies in this, that you account yourself as very little and God very great. Love means giving all that you have to Him whom you love so that nothing remains to you of your own. As you tread the Path of Love, you find that the "you" in you has vanished – alone the Lord remains. It was Hafiz, who sang, "My heart is so full of the thought of the Beloved that the thought of self has disappeared from my consciousness." In another place, he says, "Betwixt the lover and the Beloved there must be no veil. Thou thyself, O Hafiz, art the veil. Get out of the way!"

Getting out of the way, the Sufi mystics sought to realise their unity with God. They loved God for His own sake, not for any reward. They sought the Giver, not His gifts. They sought God, not "experiences", nor "miracles", nor "powers". Was it not Rabia, who said, "It is the Lord of the house whom I need. What have I to do with the house?"

Having found God, they did not forsake humanity. They came and lived in the midst of men, to share with them the treasures of the Spirit, which have been given them. Their ideal was to be *in* the world but not *of* the world. One thing only they insisted upon, "Never forget God!"

They lived ever united to the Beloved. In that union, they beheld the Light, nothing but the Light. And wherever they turned, they found God, nothing but God. They became the "Friends of God". They met Him, face to face, and saw Him "unveiled within the abode of Peace".

The world, today, is smitten with hatred between creeds and classes and countries. We are passing through a period of darkness, and each day the darkness deeper grows. What the sad world needs, today, is the living light of love. With it are illumined the lives of the "Friends of God". For they touched the depths where no separation exists, where East and West unite. In this unity is still the hope of a broken, bleeding humanity.

J. P. Vaswani

FRIENDS OF GOD

[1]

"What is Sufism?" asked a Sufi saint. And he answered, "Its beginning is God and, as regards the end, it has no end!"

The emphasis of the Sufi is on the heart. "Consult thy heart," said the Prophet of Islam, "and thou wilt hear the secret ordinance of God, proclaimed by the heart's inward knowledge, which is real faith in the Life Divine!" In many of the *suras* (verses) of the *Qur'an* and of the sayings of Muhammad, I see the beauty and light of the mystical spirit.

Where is He, the Lord of Life referred to, again and again in the *Qur'an*, as "Allah"? In answer, I read the words which I have repeated in my heart:

> Allah is in the East,
> And Allah is in the West:
> Wheresoever ye turn,
> There is the face of Allah!

And with whom is He? I read, "Allah is with those who patiently endure!"

And who are the truly spiritual? I read:

> Not they who, in their prayers, turn their heads
> To East or West, but they who believe in Allah
> And in the Angels and the Scriptures and the Prophets.
> And who give of their wealth to the poor ones,
> And to the orphans and the wayfarers.

And what should we spend in charity? I read, "All that you have left over above your needs."

The Vedas, the *Upanishads* and the *Gita* thrill with the thought that "He, the Eternal, is One", though "the sages call Him by many names." This thought of the "Unity of God", this doctrine of "God as the sole Reality", speaks to us, again and again, in the teaching of Muhammad. "He is God alone, God, the Eternal," are the words I have loved to meditate upon again and again. Listen to the mystical call of the Spirit to the human heart – in the following words of the *Qur'an*:

> Truly your God is but one!
> And He is the Lord of the Heavens and of the Earth,
> And of all that lies between them,
> And the Lord of the horizon!
>
> His, verily, is whatsoever is
> In the Heavens and on the Earth,
> And whatsoever is between the two!
> He knoweth the secrets of men's hearts
> And what is yet more hidden!
>
> And He is the Primal Light –
> The Light of the Heavens and the Earth.
> His Light is like a niche in which shines a lamp –
> The lamp within a glass:
> And the glass is like unto a bright, shining star!
>
> He is Light upon light!
> He is the Light of light!
> And the Light is adored by all!

Again, "Blessed is the man who hath kept his soul pure!"

In the revelation of the rishis, the prayer is breathed out, again and again, "Lead us, O Lord, from darkness into light." And in the mystical revelation of Islam, I read the words, "God shall bring us out of darkness into Light!" In the "traditions", there is a saying ascribed to the Prophet, it runs thus:

> God hath said, 'I am present when My servant thinks of Me!
> 'I am with Him when He remembers Me!
> 'Whosoever seeks to approach Me by a span, I will seek to approach him by a cubit.
> 'And he who seeks to approach Me by a cubit, I will seek to approach him by two fathoms.
> 'And whosoever walks towards Me, I will run towards him.'

In the teaching of Muhammad, the emphasis is on the thought that to attain to wisdom, knowledge, to the mystic gnosis—called *ma'rifa* in the Sufi books – you must be pure. What the Hindu books call *dharma*, is referred to, in the teaching of the Prophet, as "righteousness"; and righteousness, we are told, is, in essence, purity. "Happy is he," we read, "who is purified and who remembereth the Name of his Lord and prayeth." I recall a similar thought, sung again and again, in *Sri Sukhmani Saheb*, the great classic of the Sikhs:

> Remember Him!
> Remember Him,
> And have the highest bliss!

"Let thy heart be pure," saith the Prophet of Islam. The pure heart is free from "stain", and he who would be saved, must "come to God with a pure heart." In a "tradition" we are told that the Prophet often said, "There is a polish for everything that becomes rusty, and the polish for the heart is remembrance of God."

"Let thy heart be pure!" said Muhammad, again and again. The Sufi *fakir*, like the Hindu *rishi*, was led on to the practice of meditation and contemplation. When, through meditation and contemplation, the servant of God draws nigh to the Divine Life, a new love fills his heart. I recall the words attributed to Jesus in an Islamic tradition: "Jesus saith, 'Verily, if, when I come unto the innermost shrine of My servant, I find therein no love of this world or the next, then I fill him with love for Me, and hold him safely as My friend."

"My servant," we read in another tradition, "is always seeking to approach Me, so that I love him. And when I love him, I am his hearing by which he hears, I am his sight by which he sees, I am his hand by which he grasps, and I am his feet by which he walks."

So is the soul transformed. Being purified, more and more, the soul is emptied of the "ego" and attains what the Sufis call *fana*, which is "passing away" of the lower self, and enters into *baqa*, the Eternal that ever *is*. "Blessed is he", saith a Sufi sage, "who has passed away from himself, has passed away from everything except the One." The Sufi poet, Jami, sings:

> I pass away!
> Thou alone dost endure!

"When knowledge (*ma'rifa*) comes upon thee," says the great Sufi thinker, Ibn al-Arabi, "thou understandest that thou knowest God by God, not by the self." Then you attain to the state of "intoxication", of which Sufi seers have sung in rapturous strains. Then, from the servant's "tongue of exultation", saith the Sufi poet, Iraqi, is heard the secret:

> I am Love-intoxicated,
> And I sing in all tongues,
> Thy Love: Thy Love, I choose!
> And from love to Thee
> I lay down my life for Thee!

[2]

Sufism in Arabia grew out of a group of Arab ascetics whom the Prophet highly honoured. They were called *"Ahl al-suffa"*, i.e. the "People of the Bench". About three hundred in number, they were not engaged in merchandise, nor did they keep flocks. They were on terms of intimacy with the Prophet, who was glad that they ate their food in the mosque and slept there. They were ill-clad; they had no home; they sat on the stone benches outside the mosques and received alms, spending their time in devotion to God.

These men of poverty and purity were greatly admired by the Prophet. Many of the sayings of the Prophet, treasured by tradition, indicate the spiritual kinship between Muhammad and these "poor people", whose thought and life influenced not a few in Arabia. Like them, the Sufis practised meditation and lived a life of poverty and simplicity, and they believed in serving God and man.

Many of the Prophet's sayings reveal the spiritual kinship between him and the Sufis. Here are some sayings gathered from the *Hadith*, the "traditions" of the Prophet:

> The best of charity is what the right hand gives and the left hand does not know.
>
> *
>
> Charity is the duty of every Muslim. It matters little if he has nothing to give; let him do a good deed. Every good act is charity.
>
> *
>
> God does not care for the keeper of the fast who does not abandon lying and slander.
>
> *
>
> He is not a true Muslim who eats his fill and lets his neighbour go hungry.
>
> *
>
> What is the essence of religion? Purity of speech and charity.
>
> *
>
> All God's creatures are His family.
>
> *
>
> Give the labourer his wages before his perspiration is dry.
>
> *

Go in quest of knowledge even to the ends of the earth.
*
Know thyself, if thou wilt know God!
*
The key to Paradise is prayer; the key to prayer is purification.
*
The love of the world is the root of all evil.
*
Be in the world like a pilgrim, like a traveller or passer-by.
*

The Sufis were called the "friends of God" to whom was granted *ma'rifa*, the mystic "knowledge" given to those whose intuition was developed – intuition, not reason or philosophic understanding. Al-Ghazali, one of the greatest thinkers of Islam, denied that "reason" or "philosophy" could fathom the Infinite. Intuition or inward experience alone could apprehend Truth–the one Reality referred to as Wisdom, as Light, as Beauty, as Love Divine. Intuition is the inner sense, the spiritual sense—as distinguished from the physical senses. So taught the *Upanishads*, centuries before the Sufis developed the esoteric or inner side of Islam.

The spiritual sense or intuition opens inwardly and apprehends the Truth at first hand. Western mystics have referred to intuition as the eye of the Soul, and the ear of the inmost Self. Intuition beholds the Light unchangeable, the inward Light. Ekhart refers to it as the Divine Spark, which, through all the vicissitudes of life, is still knit with the Eternal Flame – the Life Divine, which is at the heart of the world.

He who would behold the Kingdom of God must be re-born. This re-birth is not possible unless purity is awakened, and this demands that the tumult of the senses is stilled and the soul stripped of the veils of selfishness and sensuality. All self-seeking, all self-will, must cease. The *Gita* refers to it as self-surrender to the Divine Will—the One Perfect Good, the Holy. So doth the seeker become *nitya-mukta* (the Ever-Free), pure from the ego, as flame is free from smoke, and crossing the stage of *fana*, the seeker passeth out of himself into the Beloved.

The one thing common to the Sufis was the austerity and simplicity of their lives. An early writer on Sufism says, "The Sufis have, for the sake of God, turned aside from all that might distract them from Him. They are content with little in the way of worldly goods and are satisfied with the least that is necessary in the way of clothing and bedding. They choose poverty rather than riches, embracing want and avoiding plenty. They renounce dignity and honour and rank, and show compassion to mankind and humility towards all. They abstain from the pleasures of the carnal self and fight against it: they know that the chief of a man's enemies is within himself."

The wandering bards in Bengal and the *fakirs* and *dervishes* in Sind, sang this truth:

> O Gangaram!
> Be simple!
> Then alone will vanish all your doubts!

[3]

There are, in the *Qur'an*, wonderful sayings, in which I see the first beginnings of the faith which developed into Sufism. "Every nation has its prophet," is a deep, mystical saying. In another passage, I read, "There is no compulsion in religion." The history of Islam would have been different, if the theologians of Islam had been true to the teaching enshrined in these words. Again, "Not a leaf falls but Allah knows it!" Again, "God is witness enough between you and me." "Three persons speak not together, but He is their fourth."

In another passage, we have the words, "If all the trees on earth were pens, if the sea with seven more seas were ink, they would still not suffice to sing the glory of God!" In yet another passage, we read:

> Did He not find you an orphan, and gave you a home?
> Did He not find you lost, and showed you the way?
> Did He not find you needy, and enriched you?

The songs of the Sufi *fakirs* are filled with this aspiration to the life of the simple way—with this vision of the One, seeing whom you fear none at all but in all situations exclaim, "All glory to my Guru – the Master!" When a Brahmin-disciple was told that he had lost his place in his community because of his devotion to a Sufi *dervish*, the disciple said:

> Let them say what they will.
> I pursue my simple way, fearing none at all!

In this "simple way", you rise above rites and creeds, above pilgrimages and ceremonies. One of the *dervishes* of East Bengal sings:

> I would not go, my heart, to Mecca or Medina!
> For, behold! I ever abide by the side of my Friend!
> Mad would I be, if I dwelt afar, not knowing Him!
> What worship may I offer in mosque or temple?
> At every step I have my Mecca and Kashi.
> Sacred to me is every moment!

This simple religion of the Sufi, wandering *fakir,* is the timeless faith, the religion of all time, the *Sanatana Dharma* of the Hindu heart. It is the religion of the *Gita* and the *Upanishads* – the religion of Krishna and the Christ. In this religion, Man is the Temple wherein—as we read in the *Upanishads*—"the very Gods came and took shelter." It is the "religion of the Heart" which gently says, "The Guru is within."

"The voice from the depths," says a Sufi *dervish*, "tells thee that the Guru is in the lotus of the Heart." As Kabir sang, "The Supreme Self the Guru, abideth near to thee. Awake! Awake! O my heart, awake!"

This awakening of the heart opens the door to the Higher Self–the *Atman*. Every path, then, as Kabir says, becomes a path of pilgrimage. Every work becomes worship – becomes service. Then, "all the world," in the words of a *fakir*-singer of God, "becomes the *Veda*, all creation becomes the *Qur'an*. Then you rise above paper-scriptures; then you gather ever fresh wisdom from the universe. Then you see that the Wisdom Eternal shines in the millions of humanity. Then your simple song has its thirty million strings, whose mingled symphony ever sounds within you. Then you take into yourself all the creatures of the world and you are lost in the one eternal Music of Man!"

Song after song of Kabir, the weaver-singer of the Mystery that is God, sounds this Sufi note, again and again. Listen to one little song:

> In every abode the Light doth shine.
> If, indeed, you cannot see,
> Then know that you are blind!
> Learn to look! Look on!
> And you will see, at last, the Light!
> Verily, then will break your bondage of death!

In another little song, this great mystic, born in a Muslim home, sings:

> Within thy body is the Garden of Paradise.
> Within thy body are the seven seas and the myriad stars.
> Within thy body is the Mystery made manifest!
> Within thy body are the Temples of the Gods,
>   And all the pilgrimages!

Another Muslim mystic, Dadu, sings:

> This body is my scripture,
> Wherein I read the message
> The All-Merciful has written for me!

Yet another mystic, Dadu's Muslim disciple, Rajab, sings:

> Within the bhakta's heart
> Is the paper on which are writ,
> In letters of life,
> The scriptures of God!
> But few, alas, do care
> To read the sacred scrolls:
> Men see not and hear not:
> They turn, alas, a deaf ear
> To the Message of the Heart!

[4]

In the Sufi programme of life, importance is given to meditation and charity, to humility and meekness, and to poverty and obedience to the *murshid* or the spiritual director. Poverty and the simple life may be seen in the work and worship of Sufi *fakirs* and *dervishes*. Not without reason were the Sufis drawn to Jesus, who had no house of his own to live in, who laid not up for the morrow and who, when night overtook him, slept where he happened to be. Muhammad is reported to have said to a disciple, "Put your trust in God and He will give you sustenance as He gives it to the birds: they come out hungry in the morning, but return full to their nests."

The love of poverty, which some of the Sufis had, recalls that of St. Francis of Assisi. In the *Ishopanishad*, the Rishi gives the teaching – *"Ma gridah!*, "Covet not!" And the Sufi *dervishes* are never tired of telling their disciples that, if they would grow in spiritual life, they must covet nothing in this world or the next, but give themselves entirely to God and turn their face to Him. "Love poverty," said Rabia, "if you will be near the Lord."

Ibrahim Adham was the King of Balkh. He renounced his kingdom and lived a life of poverty, earning his daily bread by manual labour. He met a man, who often complained, saying, "Sad is my condition: I am so poor!"

Ibrahim said to him, "My son! Perhaps you paid but little for your poverty."

"I do not understand you," said the man. "Does any one buy poverty?"

Ibrahim answered, "For my part I chose poverty and I bought it at the price of my kingdom. When I found this precious thing—poverty—I bade a final farewell to my kingship. I give thanks for my poverty. The bird of my heart has, through poverty, attained to fellowship with God."

Simple life, say the Sufi, is the essence of the wisdom of the heart. How superior it is to the knowledge of books! The great Sufi poet of Sind says:

> Be simple! Be pure!
> See the play in thy heart of Aliph (Allah),
> And thou wilt know the vanity of riches and book-learning.
> Thou wilt learn to look on life with the pure eye,
> Thou wilt know that the Name of Allah is enough.
>
> Why multiply desires?
> And why multiply these leaves of books?
> Turn over twenty, if thou wilt,
> The central word is One!
> Read thou, the One Word of Aliph, the Allah!
> And forget other leaves!
>
> O, be simple! Keep the heart pure!
> How many pages canst thou read
> If thy heart be not pure?
> They who have longing in their heart,
> They read only the page wherein they see their Beloved!

The longing to commune with the Beloved makes me what I am—an unworthy servant of my Master. Years ago, the question arose within me, "What am I?" I answered it in diverse ways. I wrote:

What am I?
An earthen lamp:
But the light that therein shines is Thine!

What am I?
Iron transmuted:
And the transmuting stone is Thine!

What am I?
A little scroll:
But the letter of Love is Thine!

What am I?
An inkpot:
But the ink of *gnana* is Thine!

What am I?
A reed:
But the flute-song is Thine!

What am I?
A streamlet:
But all the healing waters are Thine!

What am I?
A wavelet:
But its source—the sea—is Thine!

What am I?
A weather-beaten boat:
But the compass and the Captain are Thine!

What am I?
A little spark:
But the Central Flame is Thine!

What am I?
A coloured kite:
But the thread that holds me high is Thine!

What am I?
A hawker from door to door:
But all the wares are Thine!

What am I?
A servant of servants:
But the *tapas* and strength of service are Thine!

What am I?
A wandering fakir, a singer in the street:
But the Song in all the songs is Thine!

[5]

The key to meditation is this opening of the Heart to Him – the Beloved – and His holy ones. "I cannot live without Thee," said the Sufi poet, Nuri. "Thy Hand is everywhere. How long, my heart's Beloved? No more can I endure this banishment!" In meditation, the servant aims at being detached from everything but God and the *murshid* (the Guru).

The servant makes his heart a mirror. Then, into the Heart he looks, first polishing off the rust that stains the inner Self. Then, quickened by the breath of the holy ones and the Holy Spirit in the Heart, he is purified and becomes poor in spirit, and, in deep humility, he stands, at last, to gaze at the King of Beauty.

Transformed thus, the servant learns to love every one, even his "foes". And he is freed from pride: as Sri Chaitanya repeatedly asked his disciples to learn, he learns: from the tree which rewards the stone-thrower with fruit – and from every stone and every star. He heals the smiter; he blesses him who would kick or crucify!

And then? "Then, O Qasim, silence!" sings a Sufi *fakir*. Then enter into communion with the One, who is, also, the "One-many"–the "Nameless". In that beautiful poem of Tennyson, *The Ancient Sage*, I hear the blended voice of the Sufi singer, the Hindu *rishi* and the Christian mystic:

> If thou wouldst hear the Nameless and descend
> Into the temple-cave of thine own self,
> There, brooding by the central altar, thou
> Mayst happily learn the Nameless truth
> By which thou wilt abide, if thou be wise.
> For "knowledge" is the swallow on the lake,
> That sees and stirs the surface-shadow there
> But never yet hath dipt into the Abyss!

"Surface-knowledge" and "creed" have but a small place in the deeper life of the soul. Not the intellect, not theology, not ritualism, but the Heart touches the Divine Centre of Life. A Sufi singer of my native land sings:

> From all thy learned lore
> Stand thou far!
> Consider how in thee may grow
> The yearning for the Only Love!

The yearning for "Verity"–for the "Only Love"–is it not above "knowledge"? So the Sufi singers have taught that "God is beyond knowledge." Indeed, you know Him by loving Him and you love Him by dwelling in love on His Forms and His promptings in the heart. In man is God, God is in all, and all is in God. God is Love–the Only Love. I sing in my heart, again and again, the song of the Sufi poet:

> Lo here! Lo there!
> I only remember
> Thy picutre–
> Thy picture, Love!

Are not the dawn and the dusk, the sunrise and the sunset, too, His pictures?

The deeper note sounded by Sufi singers in their thought and life is—Blend love and renunciation, let the twain be one. Verily, the love of God cannot be kindled in a heart that loves comfort. Naked, the swimmer dives into the sea to find a pearl, and he who would find the "pearl of great price", should live in this world, stripping himself of comfort and pleasure. Kabir sings:

> When love and renunciation flow together
> As flow the Ganges and the Jamuna
> There is the sacred ghat (bathing-place), named
> Prayaga (the Union Supreme).

In the strain of a true Sufi, sang the *fakir*, Jaga, when he exclaimed,

> Listen, O Madha!
> Penance and creed,
> Fasting and pilgrimage,
> Reading and scholarship—
> All, all are futile.
> The end supreme is gained
> When the two streams
> Of love and renunciation
> Mingle, flowing together into the sea!

From the mingling of the two, arises inward Light: it leads the pilgrims on! They who love God find their rest in God alone. And loving God, they go forth to serve and heal their brothers and sisters in suffering and pain. To them, saith a great Sufi poet, is uttered the word of God:

> O ye who are my witnesses!
> If any comes to you sick,
> Because he hath lost me,
> Heal him!

If a fugitive from My service
Comes to you,
Bring him back!

If any comes to you,
Healer be thou and my comfort give:
Remind him that My Name endures,
For I am Love!

Verily, I am your best Physician,
For I am gentle,
And He who is gentle takes as His servants
Only those who are gentle.

RABIA: MIRA OF ISLAM
"Alone with the Beloved!"

[1]

Rabia was one of the early Sufis of Islam. She is often spoken of as Rabia Basri–from her birthplace, Basra. She rose above the limitations of *shariat*—above the credal conception of religion. She assimilated in her life the essence of true Islam which is "surrender to Allah" or dedication to the Peace and Love of God.

Some of those who belonged to the class of early Sufis were (1) Ibrahim Adham, (2) Fudayl bin Iyad, (3) Hasan of Basra, and (4) Rabia.

Ibrahim Adham was the king of Balkh. When he moved out, we are told, forty golden scimitars and forty golden maces were borne in front of him and behind him. He suddenly, renounced his throne in obedience to a Voice which cried to him as he went out, hunting, "Awake! Wert thou created for this?"

He became a *dervish* of God, earning his livelihood for some time by working as a gardener and teaching the truth, "Glorify His Name and know that His love is higher than all the eight Paradises."

Fudayl bin Iyad was at first a captain of robbers. He, too, became a dervish in obedience to a Voice which came to him, one night:

> Dost thou believe?
> Then repent! Repent!
> And give thy heart to God!

Hasan of Basra was found by his friend weeping and when asked, "Why do you weep? You are a scholar, well-versed in Law," he said, "I weep for fear I have spoken some word which is unpleasing to God." Hasan became a famous preacher of the Word of God. He dedicated his life to the service of the Eternal.

Rabia, born in a very poor family, was in life and spirit, simple, humble, childlike and unworldly. Rabia prayed without ceasing. She was absorbed in the Love for God. In silence, in prayer and meditation, her soul communed with the Unutterable. The cry of her heart was:

> O God! My God!
> O Thou, Beloved!
> Unseen but certain –
> Thou art my God,
> My All!

She was bathed in the love of the Beloved, and in her life of contemplation, prayer and fellowship with the poor, she grew beautiful "beyond the beauty of the evening star or the dawn." She went beyond the teaching of orthodox Islam—did she not learn in the School of the Holy Spirit?

Rabia's life was not colourful. It was dedicated to the service of God and man. The story of Muslim states would have been different if, indeed, they had listened to the call of mystics like Rabia and the Sufi teaching of Peace and Love. Then would the beauty of Islam have shone radiant in all the Eastern countries:

> I pray the prayer Easterners do:
> May the peace of Allah abide with you!
> Wherever you stay, wherever you go,

> The beautiful palms of Allah grow.
> Through days of labour and nights of rest
> The Love of Allah make you blest!
> So I touch my heart as the Easterners do:
> The Peace of Allah abide with you!

The beauty of Rabia's life called many to the One Lord—to *Rabb*, as He is called in Islamic scriptures. Some of Rabia's disciples saw her enveloped in Light – and she became a Light unto many. Many regarded her as a vehicle of the message of God. She herself believed that God spoke to her. Rabia had illumination from the Divine Spirit. She beheld Him in her heart, and her highest joy was to live in fellowship with Him and call Him the "Beloved".

An inspired poet of the West sang:

> God sends His teachers unto every age,
> To every clime and every race of men.

Rabia was one such Teacher to her People in the Islamic world.

Farid 'ud-Din Attar, the author of the *Memoirs of the Muslim Saints*, speaks of her as a "spotless woman" filled with a longing to be "consumed in His glory". She lived a life of extreme poverty: she became one of the greatest ascetics of Islam. But in her heart was the joy of a true saint of God. "God! My God! Thou art enough for me!" she said, again and again. It is the cry, also, of Hindu mystics and Christian Saints: it is the cry of the noblest men and women in all the religions of the world:

> No want but the want of God:
> No gain but the gaining of God:
> No loss but the loss of God:
> No knowledge but the knowledge of God!

To this truth did Rabia bear witness for almost eighty years. She lived, every day, in an atmosphere of *tawakkul*, resignation or surrender to the Will of God. The Prophet of Islam taught that the secret of true religion was submission to the Divine Will. This submission, the *Gita* calls surrender, taking refuge, *saranam,* at His Lotus Feet.

Rabia's *tawakkul* emphasises the thought that everything belongs to Him: so, may the secular be sanctified by being surrendered to Him to whom it really belongs. Rabia's *tawakkul* was blended with her spirit of prayer. To Rabia, prayer was not mere asking, it was communion with God.

Rabia rose above creeds, above all *shariat,* above all legal conception of religious life. She rose above *shariat* to that true Love which aspires to God with no motive either of gaining Paradise after death or avoiding Hell. Rabia's prayer was the aspiration to move in God's Presence, and she adored Him as the Beautiful. In one of her prayers she says:

> If I worship Thee, Lord, from fear of Hell, burn me in Hell!
> If I worship Thee for hope of Paradise, shut against me the gates of Paradise!
> But if, indeed, I worship Thee for Thine own sake, so bless me that I may abide in communion with Thine Eternal Beauty.

This communion is the state of contemplation in which is annihilated your ego or self-hood. This annihilation (*fana*) is the passing away of the individual in the Being Universal. From *fana* you pass into *baqa* – you abide in the Eternal. This mystical doctrine of *fana* was first taught by the great mystic, Bayazid of Bistam, who learnt it from his teacher, Abu Ali of Sind.

Rabia passed from the ascetic and meditative life at last to the unitive life of Love. "He loveth them and they love Him," are the words uttered by the Voice in the great Scripture of Islam. And these words are the basis of the Sufi doctrine of the Heart – the doctrine of Love. In a profound sense,

Love *is* the voice of the Heart. To one of his followers, the Prophet, we are told, said thus, "Consult thy Heart and thou wilt hear the Secret of God proclaimed by the Heart's inward knowledge."

In the "Sayings" recorded of Rabia, there is a deep yearning for God. Here are some of them:

> I have made Thee the Companion of my heart.
>
> *
>
> The groaning and the yearning of the lover of God
> Will continue until the heart has found
> Its rest in the Beloved.
>
> *
>
> The Beloved of my heart is the Guest of my soul.
>
> *
>
> My Peace is in solitude, but my Beloved is ever with me.
>
> *
>
> Nothing can take the place of His Love:
> It is the test for me among mortal beings.
>
> *
>
> O Healer of souls!
> The heart feeds upon its aspiration:
> I aspire towards union with Thee:
> And this aspiration heals my soul.
>
> *
>
> My hope is for Union with Thee.
> This Union is the goal of my quest!
>
> *

Is not the light of yearning, the light of Love—of *mahabba*—as the Sufis call it? "But they that noble are and wise," says a Muslim singer, "look unto God with yearning eyes!"

Rabia was not blind to the beauties of the outer world. Even a balde of grass or a grain of sand reflects the Infinite. Richer by far, to Rabia, was God's revelation in the Heart within. She beheld in her Heart, "the beauty which far transcends the beauties of the outward world." To Rabia, Nature was the handiwork of the Beloved who breathes His benediction in the Heart within. A Sufi *bhakta* (lover) hath well exclaimed:

> O God!
> I never hearken to voices of the animals,
> Or the rustle of the leaves,
> Or the splashing of waters,
> Or the song of birds,
> Or the whistling of the wind,
> Or the rumble of thunder,
> But I sense in them
> A testimony to Thy Unity
> And a proof that Thou art
> The All-pervading One,
> The All-knowing One,
> The All-wise, the All-just,
> And the All-true,
> For ever and evermore!
>
> O God!
> I acknowledge Thee
> In the proof of Thy acts!
> Grant me, then,
> To remember Thee
> In my love for Thee
> And in Thy love for me
> For Thou dost love me
> As Father loveth His child!

[2]

I often call Rabia the "Mira of Islam." Mira was a queen, Rabia a poor orphan. But Mira renounced her palace and all her possessions and became poor in the service of God. Both Mira and Rabia sang songs rich in *bhakti* (devotion). Both were mystics – a mystic is in tune with the Infinite. Both Mira and Rabia were God-intoxicated. Attar, a name linked with the great Sufi mystics like Ghazali, Rumi and Hafiz, speaks of Rabia in the following words:

> Veiled was she in the veil of purity:
> On fire was she with love and longing for God:
> Filled was she with the aspiration to be consumed
> in His glory:
> Lost was she in union with the Divine:
> Set apart was Rabia in the seclusion of holiness:
> Accepted was she by men as a second spotless Mary!

Born at Basra about in 717 A.D., Rabia died in A.D. 801. She was born of humble parents. She was a little girl when her mother died. Rabia was the fourth sister in the family. All members of the family were scattered by a famine. Rabia was kidnapped and sold as a slave for six *dirhams* (silver coins). Her master gave her hard work to do. Alas! He beat her, again and again. Rabia ccomplained not: patience is a mark of a true Sufi. Rabia fasted in the day to find time to cope with her work. She slept a few hours only.

Her master continued to be cruel to her. One day, she ran away. She had not proceeded far when she fell and broke her left hand. In deep agony, she cried to God:

> O Lord!
> My gracious Lord!
> Thou knowest
> I have no father:
> I have no mother:
> I am an orphan.
> As a prisoner
> I spend my time,
> Day and night, in suffering and pain:
> And now my left hand, too, is broken!
> Is it that Thou, my Divine Master,

> Art not pleased with me?
> Tell me, Lord!
> Why art Thou angry with me?

In this hour of her agony, a Voice spoke to her from within:

> My child!
> Cast all thy care on Him
> Who speaketh to thee—thy Lord!
> Soon will thy suffering be over,
> But thy witness will stand
> Before the pure ones of the Earth!

She returned to her master's house.

One night, her master happened to look down through a window of the house and saw Rabia in prayers. He listened. He heard her praying thus:

> O Lord!
> Thou knowest—
> Thou knowest all!
> Thou knowest the aspirations of my heart!
> Thou knowest I long to obey Thee!
> Thou knowest the light of my eyes
> Is in the service of Thy Holy Feet!
> If, indeed, the matter rested with me,
> I should not cease even for an hour to serve Thee.
> But it is Thy will that I be a slave to a creature,
> And much of my time is spent in his service!

The master heard Rabia's touching words and was moved. He looked up: he saw that above her head was shining a lamp suspended without a chain. He saw her enveloped in light. He saw, too, that the whole house was illuminated by a mysterious Light.

The master was deeply impressed: he was afraid, too, at the sight. He said to himself "Grievously have I sinned. I have made a Saint of Allah a slave in my house!"

He realised that Rabia was one of God's elect. He repented. And early in the morn, he went to her and said, "O thou, whom God hath blessed! I knew thee not. God in His mercy opened my eyes last night. I saw thee at prayer. I will not let thee serve me any longer. Stay in my house and be happy. Let *me* serve thee!"

Rabia said, "My master! You have given me food for so many days. I feel grateful. I now ask of thee one thing only—freedom. Be merciful to me and let me go where I will, and serve my God in freedom."

[3]

There are three types of men (and women):
1. There are men of the world: their life is centred in the little "self". They are indifferent to the realities of religion.
2. There are men who build life in "reason". They argue, they think of God in terms of His attributes and His manifestations in Nature. These men are intellectual, logical. They, too, render service to the cause of religion.
3. There are men of the mystical temperament. They are children of the Spirit. They perceive God intuitively. Their goal is ecstatic union with the Life Divine.

Rabia belonged to the third type.

She believed in meditation and prayer. Her prayer was not merely a fixed formula—an obligatory prayer at an appointed hour. Rabia's prayer was an unceasing, silent intercourse with God. This prayer, in Islam, is called *dhikr*, i.e. continuous repetition of the Name of God. In Vaishnava literature, this is called *"Hari-Nam":* the true Vaishnava repeats it in his *kirtan* again and again. How often did not Haridas repeat the Divine Name everyday, before he ate his meals! Sri Chaitanya and his devoted followers purified the atmosphere of Nadia, and, later, of Jagannath Puri, by repeated utterance of the Divine Name – *"Hari bol! Hari bol!"* ("Sing the Name of the Lord!"

And Rabia practised *tawakkul*–trust in the Lord. Your "intellectual" man reasons and says, "Money must be earned in order that the needs of life may be fulfilled." The child of the Spirit works, yet believes that God is the great Giver. The mystic looks up to Him in daily life and, even when ill, believes that medical aid itself will not do good unless blessed by the Divine Spirit. Rabia was poor: she accepted poverty as God's gift to her. Her friends often offered her material help again and again. She said again and again, that there was One who looked after her, helped her and healed her. She said:

> Verily, I ask not for worldly things from Him to whom the world belongs. I ask not, for I know He does for me what is always for my good.
> How then should I ask for worldly things from men to whom the world does not belong?

"The best thing for the servant who desires to be near the Lord," said Rabia, "is to possess nothing in this world or in the next–nothing save the Lord." She coveted no Paradise. Not in fear of hell, not in desire of Heaven, but in pure aspiration to commune with God was the secret, she taught, of true worship.

One of her friends went in her old age to her house one day and found there only four things – (1) a mat, (2) a screen, (3) an earthenware jug for water, and (4) a bed which served, also, as her prayer-carpet.

She believed in renunciation as a law of spiritual life. Remarkable was her asceticism. When one of her acquaintances suggested that he would ask some of his kinsmen to get her a servant who would do the work of her house – sweep the floor, cleanse the utensils, fill the water jug for her, she said, "The whole world belongs to my Divine

Master, and He will do for me what He knows is the best for me. Trust in God," she said "What He does for you is the best for you!"

One day, a friend (Hasan of Basra) came to visit her. He saw a wealthy merchant of Basra at the door of Rabia's cell with a purse of gold: the merchant stood at the door, weeping.

"Why do you weep?" asked Hasan.

The merchant said, "Rabia is the great ascetic of this age: if she were not in our midst, we would perish. Her blessings sustain us and keep us alive. Alas! She lives in extreme poverty. I have brought for her a little gold! My fear is, she may tell me, 'Take it back. I want nothing!' If you will be so good as to plead for me, she may be pleased to accept my offer."

Hasan gave the message to Rabia. She looked at him and said:

> God provides for those who revile Him: will He not provide for those who love Him?
> He sustains those who speak unworthily of Him: will He not sustain me, whose soul overflows with love for Him?
> Ever since I have known Him, I have turned away from men to Him who is the Giver of all!

Rabia loved to regard herself as a "servant of the Lord." And "the servant who desires to be near to his Lord," she said, "should possess nothing in this world or the next save the Lord alone!"

[4]

Repentance, *tawakkul*, prayer and love—I regard as the fourfold treasure of Rabia.

Rabia often said that repentance (*tauba*) was the very first step on the Spiritual way. It is the first "station" in the way to the perfect life. And repentance, she taught, was a gift from

God. On one occasion, she said, "How can anyone repent unless the Lord gives him repentance and accepts him? Seeking forgiveness merely with the tongue," she said "is the sin of lying!" After repentance comes "conversion" (*inabat*). Then comes renunciation (*zuhd*).

Then comes trust in God (*tawakkul*). Rabia was poor, poverty did not frighten her. She surrendered her life to God. She feared not, for she had *tawakkul* – "God will provide!"

Prayer, said Rabia, was a free and intimate intercourse with God. Prayer was more than the prescribed *namaz* and other religious observances. In her life, she bore witness to the truth that prayer was communion with God. Every spot was, to her, sacred as a mosque, and every day the word arose in her heart, "My Beloved!" Prayer was a heart-to-heart converse with God. Prayer was spontaneous outpouring of the heart to God. Here is one of her prayers on which I have meditated again and again:

> O my Lord!
> If, indeed, Thou hast bestowed on me a share of this world, I pray to Thee to bestow it on those who deny Thee or revile Thy Name.
> And if, indeed, Thou hast decreed that I should have a share of the next world, I pray this humble prayer, "Give not the share to me, but give it to those who glorify Thee and Thy Name!"
> For Thou, O Lord, art enough for me. I need nothing else, nothing else!

Love or ecstatic vision of the Beloved–was the goal of Rabia's life. The highest aspiration of Rabia's heart is expressed in the following verses:

> Two ways I love Thee:-
> My selfish love, love of my happiness,
> And next, perfect love, the love which, indeed, is worthy of Thee.

> 'Tis selfish love that I do nought,
> Save think on Thee excluding all beside.
> But the perfect love, the purest love,
> Which is Thy Love,
> Shines forth when the veils which hide Thee fall
> And I do gaze on Thee!

Yes, the perfect love, the purest love, is illumination: in it, the veil is raised and the worshipper, the *bhakta*, the devotee sees the Beloved, face to face. In the purest love, you see the Divine Beauty and you experience mystical union with God. This mystical union is referred to in a tradition of the Prophet:

> God said, "My servant draws nigh unto Me and I love him. And when I love him, I am his ear, so that he hears by Me—and his eye, so that he sees by Me—and his tongue, so that he speaks by Me—and his hand, so that he takes by Me!"

In this love, the mystical love, the motive is not *fear* of God and of the "wrath to come" but "ecstatic communion" with the Divine.

You start then with repentance, which comes to him on whom is the grace of God. You proceed to spiritual disciplines of which an important one is renunciation or poverty. The basis of poverty is *tawakkul*, i.e. dependence on God. You grow in prayer which deepens into *dhikr*—constant repetition of the Name of Allah. So are you *purified* and gradually you rise to illumination, to gnosis (*ma'rifa*), which is knowledge and, at last, you attain to communion with God which is reflected in the lives of saints who behold the Beloved with purified hearts. When love of the heart communes with the Beloved, you reach the goal: and loving god, you grow in the love of your fellow-beings and, indeed, of all His creatures.

In the consummation of love, there is the annihilation of the I, the ego, the lower self. Your life, then, becomes a mirror of God. "You" are no more: the "I" has vanished! The aspiration, then, of the *salik*, the traveller on the Path is:

> Betwixt me and Thee,
> There lingers yet an "It is I!"
> That torments me!
> Ah! Of Thy grace, take away
> This "I" from between us!

Rabia went through spiritual disciplines in order to achieve the mystical union with God. Of this sings the great Sufi-poet of Iran:

> Happy the moment
> When we are seated
> In the palace—Thou and I!
>
> With two forms
> And with two figures
> But with one soul—Thou and I!

Pure and profound was Rabia's love for God. He was her Beloved. Her hand was sought in marriage by a number of men: she declined all offers. She said:

> Marriage! How is it possible for me?
> I have ceased to exist:
> I am no longer "I"!
> I exist in Him:
> I am altogether His!
> I live in the shadow of His command!
> Not from me,
> But from Him
> Must a man ask for me
> In marriage!

Rabia lived in the presence of the Purest One: to Him she gave herself, her heart and its purest love. And is it not true that if a man surrenders himself to Him, He – the Lord –

surrenders Himself to him? Blessed – thrice-blessed was Rabia. Bayazid, the Sufi, rightly said: "Whoever seeth a God-man is blessed: he hath conquered all ills!"

[5]

Rabia was among the earliest exponents of the Sufi Way of life and the Sufi view of Love Divine. In the Sufi Way, there are three journeys:

1. The first is "journey to God" (*sayar ila'llah*). In this journey, the *salik*, the pilgrim, the aspirant–the *jignasu*, to use a term of Hindu thought–travels from the "world of creation" to the "world of Reality," often called *Haqiqat-i-Muhammadi*.

2. The second is "journey in God" (*sayar fi'llah*). In this, the *salik*, the aspirant, is absorbed into the Divine Essence. Arriving at this stage, the Hindu seer exclaimed, "*Tat twamasi*!" "That art thou!" That–the Divine Essence–is thy Goal! That-is the one Reality wherein thou art to abide as thy Home! Well exclaimed the Muslim mystic:

   > I am in Him whom I love!
   > We are two spirits in one Body!
   > In me, see thou Him!
   > And seeing Him, well mayst thou see us both!

3. The third is "journey from God" (*sayar ani'llah*). This is the journey *back* to the world of manifestation. In the second journey, you enter into *fana*, annihilation. In the third journey, you enter into *baqa*, subsistence. You are on the plane of manifestation, yet, are established in the Eternal.

Rabia was among the first singers and interpreters of the Doctrine of the Heart. "All that eyes behold," said a Muslim mystic, "belongs to earthly knowledge, but what the heart beholds, belongs to Certainty," and therefore, to Eternity. "If you would be a true seeker," Rabia said, "go within and purify yourself, renouncing the inward sins." Going within, you will behold the Light! "Verily, knowledge is Light," said Abu Talib, "which God breathes out in the heart!"

Rabia, too, taught the Doctrine of God's Grace: it protects the seeker, and the greatest protection is his who learns to obey Him in all situations. In obeying the Will Divine is the true wisdom of life!

[6]

Like Mira, Rabia cried, again and again, "I can no longer live without Thee, Beloved!" And when she died to "selfhood", she rejoiced and cried, "Blessed am I: I am Thine, Beloved!"

Rabia, I call the Mira of Islam. Christian writers have called her the "Moslem St. Teresa". Alike Mira, Teresa and Rabia had a perception of the goal of the mystic—a perception of that Kingdom which is our Home—this earth-life being the journey of pilgrims to our true Home-land. Rabia refers to it in beautiful terms:

> Beloved!
> My aspiration is but one—
> To remember Thee and Thee alone
> Above all the things of the Earth!
> This, also, is the longing in my heart,
> That in the next world, too,
> I may meet Thee alone, face to face!

Love with Rabia was dedication—a total dedication of the will to the Will Divine, of the heart to her Source. Rightly says a mystical writer of the West, "It is the heart and never the reason which leads to the Absolute." The dedication of love, Rabia said, was *detachment*—estrangement from all worldly affection. Again and again, breathes forth in Rabia's words, the cry for love:

> Beloved! Beloved!
> I am all Thine!
> Art Thou not all mine?

Rabia had but one thought—to spend her entire life for the Beloved. Like Mira, Rabia regarded herself as a moth "burnt with the touch of the Beloved's Face". "O heart," cried a great mystic of Iran, "hasten thither! For God will shine upon you and the world will seem to you a sweet garden instead of a terror."

Rabia, like the early Franciscans, practised complete renunciation of worldly things, of fame and wealth. Rabia's poverty was an expression of her detachment from the not-God and her devotion to the one God. Attachments become centres of conflicting interest: detachment saves you from complicated life and leads you on the right path—the path of simplification. It is a great adventure this—to strip yourself of everything and rely on the only One—the Beloved!

Rabia sought God with the purest love of her heart: she sought Him not for anything extern, but only for His sake. She asked for nothing in this world, nothing in the next. Over and over again, she ejaculated, "Beloved! Thou art my all!" Her love for Him was not a superficial emotion but a dedication, a total dedication of her will and her life-force to Him and His service. Rabia's love was not an emotion, but a movement, a life-movement of her total self. In a beautiful tract by a mystic who has, like the Teachers of the *Upanishads*, withheld his name, we read the following significant words:

> Silence is not God,
> And speaking is not God!
> Fasting is not God,
> And eating is not God!

Seclusion is not God,
Company is not God!

Nor may He be found
By any work of thy soul!
He may be found alone
By love of thine heart!

Not by reason
May He be known,
And He may not be gotten
By thought,
Nor concluded by understanding!

But He may be loved and chosen
With the true lovely will
Of thine heart!

Rabia's heart was filled with longing for the Beloved. Her life had but one aspiration to serve Him and be spent in His service. Such a love is fulfilled only in the annihilation of the ego or self. Rabia's joy was only in this – that her heart might be hidden in the Heart of the Beloved.

[7]

Rabia is rightly regarded as one of the earliest Sufis. Her heart was *detached* from the world: passions were uprooted from her soul, desires were extirpated. Sannai has well observed, "Ne'er can the world and Love together go!" Rabia realised that Allah's richest revelation was in the heart of Him who loved Him. In sense experience you contact an object in space, in mystical experience you contact the Divine Life in the heart within. In this experience, the heart transcends time and space and matter and mechanism. This experience, oftener than not, cometh not in din and roar, in storm and thunder, but in a voice of stillness.

One of her companions said of her that Rabia prayed all night. She had but an interval of light sleep in her place of prayer when the day was about to dawn. Then, waking up, she would say:

> O my soul!
> How long?
> How long wilt thou sleep?
> And how often wilt thou wake?
> Death is at the door,
> And soon will the body sleep
> A sleep that will no waking know
> Until the trumpet-call
> Of the Day of Resurrection!

A companion asked Rabia, "Is there anything you would like to eat?"

Rabia said, "You know I like to eat dates. For ten years have I lived here: dates are plenty here. But I have not yet eaten a single one of them. Why? I am a servant of the One Master. The desire of the servant matters little. I can but eat or have what the Beloved wills for me!"

Rabia, indeed, had renounced everything to God. Not one thing could she call her own. Nothing belonged to her. All belonged to her Beloved. She, too, was not her own but entirely His.

When asked, "You speak of God, you worship Him. Have you seen Him?" Rabia answered, "If I see Him not, how can I worship Him? But the Beloved cannot be weighed in words!"

Filled to overflowing was Rabia's heart with love. And to the worst of sinners she gave the love of her gentle heart.

One day she was asked, "Don't you regard Satan as your enemy?"

Rabia gently answered, "In my heart is limitless love for my Beloved: and I find there is not an empty corner in my heart for enmity to anyone or desire to fight anyone. By God's grace, there is not one whom I may regard as my enemy!"

[8]

A mystic whose name is closely associated with that of Rabia was Hasan al-Basri. Both were ascetics. Both represented early Sufism. A Muslim writer of note said the following of Hasan, "Hasan was among the shining stars in learning, asceticism, virtue and devotion to God. Hasan was noted, also, for his jurisprudence and rhetoric and knowledge of the Divine things. He was, also, a noted preacher: his sermons touched all hearts."

Hasan preached every Friday and Rabia went regularly to listen to him. He preached what he and Rabia practised in life – renunciation. Many looked up to him as their *pir* or religious leader. His memory is still fragrant in Islam.

Like John the Baptist, who preached in another age and another country, Hasan asked his hearers to repent. He said:

Repent! Repent! Repent!
This life and its pleasures are transient, passing!
Repent! Repent! Repent!

Great was his reverence for Rabia. One day she was very late in coming. Hasan waited until she came. One of those present at the meeting asked him, "Sir! Why do you wait for Rabia?" Hasan answered, "Whatever light shineth in my words cometh to me from the heart of Rabia."

We are told that Hasan hearing, one day, of a man who said he would be happy if, even after a thousand years in Hell, he would be saved in the end, Hasan burst into tears!

They asked Hasan, "Why do you weep, O preacher of the Word of God?"

He answered breifly, "O, that I, too, might say like that man: I shall be God's at last and shall be saved in the end!"

Again and again, Hasan said with tears in his eyes, "Alas! I am like a man who is in the sea with an old, broken boat – trembling!"

Like Rabia, Hasan emphasised the thought that the root of religion was abstinence. Again and again, he sounded the note:

> Restrain! Restrain!
> Restrain your carnal desires!
> And remember God!

One day, Hasan asked Rabia, "Tell me how you attained to this spiritual height."

Rabia answered, "I know not where I stand: I only know that I did but one thing, friend! I scattered all I received."

Yes, Rabia realised that life was given not to hoard but to scatter in the service of her Beloved.

One day, Hasan asked Rabia, "Tell me what is God." Rabia said:

> He is as He is!
> And you know it.
> I think of Him in two ways thus:
> I think of Him as *arupa* and as *amapa*.
> *Arupa* is He, for He hath no form!
> *Amapa* is He, for He is Infinite, Measureless!

So thought, too, the great Sufi, Bayazid, when he compared God to the Sea that rolls on, unexhausted and unlimited. Bayazid said, "God is an unfathomable ocean!"

"Don't you desire Paradise?" Rabia was asked. And she answered: "It is the Lord of the House I need: what have I to do with the House?"

Speaking, one day, to his congregation concerning the Way to God, Hasan said:

> Blessed is he who needs nothing, for he will have all!

> Blessed is he who is a lover of solitude, for he will find Peace!
> Blessed is he who treads under his feet the lusts of the flesh, for he will be free!
> Blessed is he who learns to endure, for he will have joy in Eternity!
> Blessed is he who spends the night awake, for he listens to the Voice that is deathless!
> Blessed is he who forgets not God at night while the tears flow down his cheeks, for he will be accepted by the Lord!

As I read these beautiful words of Hasan, I say to myself, "Is there not in them a moving picture of Rabia – a lover of the Beloved?"

[9]

A companion asked Rabia, "What is wisdom?"

Rabia said, "True wisdom is knowledge of God, and the secret of knowledge is surrender to the Will Divine."

A friend asked her: "Who among men is truly great?"

And Rabia answered: "He who has achieved four things. (1) He who has purified his heart. (2) He who with the purified heart has learnt to pray to God. (3) He who hath risen to that true prayer which surrenders all to Him in a spirit of *tawakkul*, believing that 'He will take the best care of me'. (4) He who is absorbed in meditation on Him and in singing His Name."

"Whence are you come?" they asked her.

And she said: "From the Other Shore!"

They asked her again: "Whither are you going?"

She replied: "To the Other Shore!"

"If a man possessed the whole world," they asked, "would he not be immeasurably rich?"

Rabia answered: "How could he be rich? The whole world would not make him wealthy, for the riches of the world perish and pass away."

"What do you desire?" Sufyan asked her.

Rabia answered, "I am a servant, what has a servant to do with desires? If I ask for anything which my Lord does not will, then, indeed, I am an atheist, an unbeliever! If, indeed, I would be His servant, I should will only what He, my Divine Master, wills!"

A friend said to her, "Rabia! You are so ill: much have you suffered. Why don't you pray to God for relief from illness?"

Rabia answered "O friend! Know you not who it is who wills this suffering for me? Is it not God who wills it?"

There was but one prayer in Rabia's heart, day and night, "O God! My God! Thy Will be done!"

Malik Dinar was a Sufi: he was deeply pained to find that Rabia spent her days in poverty. He met her, one day, and said to her, "Permit me, Rabia, to ask my rich friends to relieve your poverty."

Rabia looked at Malik Dinar and said:

"Your friends are rich. Is it not true that He–the One Lord–gives daily bread alike to them and to me?

Do you think He will ever forget the poor because they are poor, or remember the rich because they are rich?

Does He not know my state? Why, then, should you remind Him that I am poor?

Let us will what He wills and we shall be happy!

"Whence is Love?" they asked her, "and whither does it go?"

Rabia answered; "Love cometh from Eternity, and love is a pilgrim to Eternity!"

Someone asked her: "Don't you, sometimes, have a feeling of aversion to sinners?"

Rabia said: "Love to God has, by His grace, so possessed me, that in my heart there is no room for aversion or hate to anyone."

"What is your hope?" they asked her.

She said,

> My hope is that my aspiration may be fulfilled.
> My aspiration is Union with Him.
> It is the goal of my Desire!

Once, she fell ill: in her heart was deep longing for God. And in a moment of inward pain she exclaimed, "The healing of my wound is union with the Friend!"

A friend asked her, "How may we know that God is well pleased with His servant?"

Rabia said, "When the servant greets suffering as a gift from Him even as he would greet what he regards as good—regarding both pain and pleasure as messengers of God."

A friend asked her, "What is the deepest need of the life of him who is in quest of God?"

Rabia said, "He who would walk the Way needs neither eyes to see, nor tongue to tell. What he needs is a pure heart. So strive for purity. Then will your consciousness awake and you will no longer fall into the slumber of the senses. When the mind is truly awakened, it serves as a true friend: then, indeed, you need no other friend."

Her companion asked her: "What is meant by the awakened mind?"

Rabia answered: "One sign of the awakened mind is that it is centred in God and will not wander after anything else. The mind that is absorbed in the service of the One hath craving for nothing else."

Rabia had an awakened mind: and she had an illuminated heart. Therefore was her life rich in the mystical element of love and adoration. Her Sayings arrest our attention even today. The secret of her Sayings, as of Sri Ramakrishna's in our days, was love.

[10]

A Czech historian makes a suggestive distinction between civilisation and culture. Civilisation, he says, is everything bequeathed to us by the past, but culture, he points out, is our activity in and upon this inheritance. He points out, further, that we should so regulate our life that there should be no conflict between our inheritance and our activity.

In India, there is, alas, a conflict, a destructive conflict between the two. Our inheritance is spiritual, our activity is dominated by technical ideals. The conflict continues to grow. We tread the barren path of imitation, and our lives are becoming more and more shrunken, where we talk of economic progress and efficiency.

Under the influence of the machine, man is in process of dehumanising himself: and we see how nations fight one with the other! We cry with the Poet: "Alas! what man has made of man!" A great French thinker of our day, Marcel, deplores that we live in a "broken world". And I recall the words of a mystic of Iran:*

> Homeless am I, O Lord!
> Whither shall I turn?
> A wanderer am I, O Lord!
> Whither shall I turn?
>
> I come, driven from every threshold,
> And if thy door, too, be closed.
> Whither shall I turn?
>
> Faint are my limbs
> And feeble is my strength,
> And my heart is fearful, Lord!
> Whither shall I turn?
>
> Blessed are they who live

---

*The poem is given here with slight modifications.

In sight of Thee!
Who speak with Thee
And dwell with Thee, O Lord!
Humbly would I sit at the Feet
Of those who are dear to Thee!

Drunk, alas, with pleasure is this age:
In this drunken age,
Thou art our Faith!
Helpless are we
And weak are our hands and feet!
How can we reach Thee?
Thou art our Faith!

Christians or Muslims,
Hindus or Zarathustrians,
Whatever our country, colour or creed,
Thou art our Faith!

In these words, is the deepest cry, too, of Rabia's heart. She regarded herself as a devotee of all Prophets, all Saints, all Silent Mystics, for "all come from Thee," she said.

Need I add that Rabia's prayers, too, are most suggestive, in this connection:

O God!
My God!
I have but one desire—
To chant Thy Name
And to remember Thee
Above all the things of the earth.
And this, too, is the aspiration of my Heart
That I should, here, and in the world beyond this world,
Meet Thee, face to face,
And only chant, "Thy Will be done!"

*

> O my Joy!
> The Desire of my Heart!
> O my Friend,
> My Life and my Love!
> My Beloved!
> If only Thou
> Be well pleased with me,
> Then am I happy, indeed.
> Beyond all measure,
> Happy at Thy Holy Feet!

Yet another prayer, very brief, very beautiful. I never read it but my eyes are touched with tears. This little prayer I am tempted to quote as I close:

> O God!
> My God!
> The stars are shining!
> And the eyes of men
> Are in slumber closed!
> The kings have shut their doors
> And every lover is alone
> With his Beloved!
> And here am I
> Alone with Thee,
> Alone with my Beloved!

ABU HASAN

*"When thy heart is filled with love,
thou wilt see God everywhere!"*

---

[1]

Abu Hasan was a true *fakir* of God. The word "fakir" has by some been derived from "fikra", which means "meditate". A true *fakir* is, essentially, a man of meditation: and a lover of poverty. Abu Hasan was a man of meditation, a teacher of truth and a servant of the poor. He was a *fakir* who regarded himself as poor in the sight of God and who rejoiced in prayer, service and the simple living.

Thinking of Abu Hasan, I have been reminded, again and again, of Jesus. There is a unity among the lovers of God. Both Jesus and Abu Hasan lived and moved and had their being in God, and God to both was an "experience", not merely an "object". Both taught the truth that to "know" God, it was necessary to be purified from the "ego", the "lower self."

"I see the universe enshrined in my body," cried Abu Hasan. The universe, referred to, is not the "lower world of darkness", but the spiritual world of "light and goodness".

And again:

> Ask for a single drop of His grace; ask for nothing else in the world!

*

> When thy heart is filled with love, thou wilt see God everywhere.

*

For him who loveth God every spot, indeed, is a mosque, and every month is holy, holy, holy!

*

Give thy life to Him and He will give His life to thee!

*

When thou wilt annihilate thyself, thou wilt be perfect!

*

Keep thy mouth shut! And when you open it, speak of nought but God!

*

Love Truth and Truth will love thee.

*

Jesus was a lover of God and a lover of man. He loved silence and was a servant of the poor. Eastern traditions are full of the "Sayings" of Jesus on which I have loved to meditate, again and again:
Speak not much except in the mention of God.

*

Every word which is not a mention of God is vain.

*

The best of all your works is the love you give to God.

*

St. John, the Disciple, in the eightieth year of his life, said to his children in Christ:

Beloved!
Let us love one another!
For love is of God:
And everyone that loveth
Is born of God,
And knoweth God.
He that loveth not,
Knoweth not God,
For God is Love!

Abu Hasan worshipped God as Love and was a lover and servant of the poor. Jesus dearly loved to be called, "O poor one!" To his disciples Jesus said, again and again: "Love ye the poor, if ye will love me truly!"

Abu Hasan, like Jesus, belonged to the City of Silence. This Sufi teacher was a man of very few words, but they were "winged" words. One of them was renunciation–which is outer and inner. Renounce the unlawful, and so be purified in the heart. And renounce desire, craving, the ego, I.

A significant thought of Abu Hasan is – detachment. The *Gita* utters, again and again the great word, "desirelessness." And Jesus said, "Blessed are the poor in spirit." So Abu Yazid, the great Sufi of Baghdad, said:

> As I came near to the Lord,
> I heard a Voice say,
>   "Ask what thou dost desire!"
>
> And I answered to the Voice thus,
>   "Thou art the Object of my desire!"
>
> Then said the Voice to me,
>   "Bayazid!
>   O Bayazid!
>   Thou canst not meet Me
>   If there remain in thee
>   One atom of thine own desire!"

On one occasion Abu Hasan said:

> And He, the Lord, did say to me,
> "Ask of Me what you will,
> And it shall be given unto you!
> Some do come to Me in quest
> Of silver and gold, and these
> I give to them, but I fain would see thee
> Come and surrender thyself to Me!"

On another occasion, Abu Hasan said to a group of seekers:

> Brethren!
> Two ways there be.
> One is a long way,
> The other is the short one.
> By the long way travels man to God.
> He goes through a cycle
> Of rites and ceremonies,
> Of writ duties,
> Of penance and scriptural reading.
> By the short way
> Travels to the seekers,
> God Himself: in Him is the longing
> To meet the man
> Who yearns to meet the Beloved!

A disciple asked:

> What does He do
> When He comes by the short road
> And greets the man of yearning?

Abu Hasan answered:

> God greets the man
> And saith with love in His heart,
>   "My child!
>   Behold! I come to thee.
>   Accept Me!"
>
> "And how may I accept Thee.
> O King of kings?"
>
> And Allah (God) answers thus,
>   "My child!
>   Accept Me as thy Beloved!
>   And so be not sad
>   To lose thyself!"

Abu Hasan further said:
> Brethren!
> This is the Law.
> He who cometh nigh to Allah
> Loseth what he hath.
> Aye, he loseth himself,
> But gains instead the Gift Supreme—
> The Gift of Humility!

So Jesus taught that the Kingdom of God came by love and lowliness of mind. It was the Kingdom of the Spirit, of which the citizens were not the worshippers of wealth, not the proud of power, not the lovers of tumults and shouts, but the poor in spirit and the meek, the humble, the cross-bearers, who, through renunciation and sacrifice, aspired to the New Life.

[2]

Abu Hasan lived in a small place named Kharka. Great was his influence on those who saw him. He was a man who subjugated his senses; it was his aspiration to become a vehicle of the Spirit.

The date of his birth is not known. But we know that he was a contemporary of Sultan Mahmud of Ghazni (in Eastern Afghanistan), who lived toward the end of the tenth century. Mahmud saw India's rich treasures across the borders. India's temples had accumulated vast quantities of gold, silver and jewelery. The Hindus, alas, had not organised their forces for the protection of their country and their wealth, their culture and freedom. About India's boundaries hovered hordes of Afghans and Turks, Huns and Scythians. And Hindus suffered from internal divisions.

Towards the end of the tenth century, Mahmud swept across the frontier with an Afghan force and attacked the Hindus at Bhimnagar. The Hindus were unprepared. We know not how many of them were slaughtered. But we know that Hindu temples were destroyed and Mahmud returned to Ghazni with treasures of jewels and pearls. And every winter Mahmud came to India and returned to Ghazni with his treasure chests filled with silver and gold.

Mathura, the city of Krishna, too, was attacked by Mahmud. He took from the Temples statues of gold and precious stones. He came again and attacked the prosperous city of Somnath. The temple-priests offered him millions of money to spare the Temple. But Mahmud was a man of blood and iron. He believed in war and violence. Under his orders, the temple-priests were ruthlessly slaughtered. Somnath, with its hoarded wealth, succumbed to the invasion of this man, who resembled Attila and Chengiz Khan! Yet, when he died, they hailed him as the "greatest sovereign of his age". He was, perhaps, the richest king of whom there is any record in history.

The memory of his cruel deeds haunts Mahmud. Bitter are the tears of repentance he sheds. An Adviser says to him, "There is a prayer of the Hindu people. Repeat that prayer again and again and you will be consoled."

And Mahmud said, "O, tell me the prayer."

The Adviser repeats the prayer:

> From the unreal lead me to the Real!
> From darkness lead me to Light!
> From death lead me to Immortality!

"Yes," says Mahmud, "this world is woven in darkness: this world is shot through and through with death! My years are wasted. I have but built a kingdom of darkness! I cry for a Kingdom of Light. I begin to realise that to love mercy is to walk the path to peace and joy."

Some days passed by. The king was again in a mood of extreme dejection. He sheds copious tears and asks the Adviser, "Is there a holy man to whom I may go and have his blessings?"

The Adviser says, "Yes, sire! Nearby is the humble dwelling of a Musim *dervish*, a true saint, a man of God."

Mahmud said, "To him, let us go, tomorrow!"

Mahmud Ghazni comes to meet Abu Hasan. At first a messenger is sent to meet the saint. The messenger says, "Servant of God! The great Sultan cometh to meet you. It is but right that you come out of your house to greet the king."

Abu Hasan says, "Brother! forgive me. Go and tell the king that Hasan is all absorbed in greeting the King of kings, and has no time to greet anyone else."

Mahmud Ghazni is amazed at this answer. His vanity was wounded. But he exercises self-control and says, "Let me see this man – and test him."

Mahmud puts off his royal robe and gives it to a companion to wear it. Mahmud, himself, put on the simple dress of a *sipahi* (soldier). The two reach the cottage of Hasan.

At the door, Mahmud gives a salute to the *dervish* who is sitting in his room. And the *dervish* seated on the ground returns the salute but does not go out to greet the king.

The *sipahi* says to Hasan, "O *dervish* of God! Your king is at the door. Rise to greet him!"

Hasan says: "These be but forms and ceremonies. A *dervish* rises above them all to commune with the Beloved. Send your servants afar, then come to me."

Mahmud now knows that Hasan knows and sends afar the servants and enters the cottage and sits at Hasan's feet.

The king says, "O *dervish*! Do explain to me what Bayazid means."

And Hasan says, "Bayazid saith, 'Whoever seeth a God-man is blessed; he hath conquered all ills.'"

"How can this be?" asks the king. "The Holy Prophet had two uncles. They were evil-minded and they saw the Holy Prophet. But their ills were beyond measure and they were in the depths of misery."

Hasan says, "O king! You speak as one who knoweth not! Only a few of his followers did really see the Holy Prophet! Thus is it written in the Holy Writ. And you forget that Allah looketh at you but you *see* Him not. God's *nazar* is upon you but you do not have a vision of Him. A God-man may *look* at you, but you may not really *see* him. Only to a few is granted the vision of a God-man, as he really is in God!"

The king is struck with this answer, and with folded hands he says, "O *dervish* of God! Teach me. For I know nothing."

Hasan says, "O king! What may I teach? (1) A king should keep away from injustice; (2) A king, with a heart contrite and lowly, should, in fellowship with the people, worship Allah everyday; and (3) A king should look upon his people with eyes of compassion and serve God by being a servant of the people."

The king's eyes are touched with tears. And bowing down in reverence, he says, "Bless me, O *dervish* of God!"

And Hasan says, "O my God! Thou art the Lord of Compassion! Forgive Thou the men who walk the way that leadeth to Thee!"

"And why?" asks the King.

"Lest they be tempted to fall in the trap of pride and think that they are a class apart from others!"

The king says, "A second blessing, too, give me thou, O *dervish* of God!"

And Hasan says, "So act everyday that your works and their fruits are praised in the Court of the Angels."

"And why?" asks the king.

"For the praise of men is flattery and is born of conceit or ignorance, but the Angels know and they praise with a clean heart and a seeing mind."

The king receives the radiation of the saint's loving heart and feels very happy. Filled with joy, he places, at Hasan's feet a gift of a thousand gold *mohurs* (sovereigns). And Hasan lays his hand upon a piece of bread, and breaks it into fragments and one fragment of it he gives to the king, saying, "Eat it!"

The king begins to chew it, but he cannot gulp it down his throat. And Hasan says to him, "O king, you are unable to swallow this fragment of bread: you find it too bitter for you. Is it not so? This bread does not go down your throat. Then tell me, O king, how can I swallow these bitter *mohurs* of gold. Take these back, O king!"

The king presses Hasan again and again to accept the *mohurs*, not one does Hasan touch.

The king rises to go.

"And now," says the king, "let me take leave of you, O *dervish* of God! I go with gratitude in my heart for your teaching and blessing. But one longing remains."

"What is it? Speak without reserve!" says Hasan.

The king says "I wish to take from you something as a token of my visit to a saint and a servant of God."

Hasan then takes a fragment of the cloth worn by him and hands it over to the king. The king's joy knows no bounds. And as the king was about to go, Hasan rises up and bids him farewell.

Then says, the king: "O *dervish* of God! When I came to you, you treated me with supreme indifference. But now, as I go, you rise up and show respect to me! What is the meaning of it all?"

Hasan says, "When you came to me, you came with the pride of a king, you came to examine me. Now you go in humility and purity and with the mercy of God in your heart. And over you shines this fragment of a fakir's *garment*, radiant with the golden Light of God! I have risen up to bow *not* to a king, but to this golden Light of the King of kings!"

[3]

Reviewing the life and teaching of Hasan, I am reminded, again and again of Jesus. He taught his disciples to close the door and pray, for the Father, who is secret, heareth in secret. Verily, Abu Hasan lived a hidden life in the Hidden Lord.

He kept away from the shouts and tumults of men, and feared not the censure of the crowds. He called popular opinion the "cackling of geese" or the "mewing of cats".

His own wife understood him not. And she criticised him before his disciples and admirers. But he reamined patient and forgiving. Not once did he complain of her to anyone. To bear and endure is ever a mark of him who would grow in the grace of God.

Hasan's humility was profound. He was sitting, one day, in a cottage, surrounded by some of his followers. A man brought to him a *maund* of flour and said, "This is my offering to those who practise *tapasya* (self-control) and renunciation."

Hasan had not taken a morsel of bread for seven days. And when the man had left, Hasan said to his followers, "This *maund* of flour is meant for those who practise *tapasya* and renunciation. Alas! I cannot touch this flour, for mine is not a life of *tapsaya* and sacrifice. Mine is a life of aspiration and longing for the Lord."

Is not humility the secret of the life of saints?

Religion, to Abu Hasan, was realisation, not the cowl of a monk, nor the ritual of a mosque.

There came to him, one day, a man who said, "Thou art a *dervish* of God. Give me the clothes thou hast worn and I shall wear them!"

And he said, "May I request you, first, to answer one question? If a man wears a woman's clothes, does he become a woman?"

"No," said the man.

And the *dervish* asked again "If a woman wears a man's clothes, does she become a man?"

"No," was the answer.

"Then," said Hasan, "how can you, by wearing a *fakir's* clothes, become a *fakir?*"

And Hasan proceeded to tell the man that he could not become a *fakir* until he had first a longing for God. In yearning was the seed of realisation.

Coarse was the cloth he wore, and simple was his food, and he owned no property. Poverty was dear to him. "Through poverty", he said, "you become free." Through poverty, you are "initiated into the Great Life of the All."

Did not Jesus say, "The love of the world corrupts the seeker. But to him who is established in God, the world is the same as a stone or a clod"?

"What is true service?" they asked Hasan. And he answered, "Every act rich in renunciation." Interpreting the thought further, he said:

> Body, speech and mind – the three are no longer mine!
> I have surrendered them to the Lord.
> And neither this world, nor the next is mine.
> My world is the Lord!

The Sufi, Mu'adh Er-Razi, said in a similar strain, "Paradise is the prison of the initiate, as this world is the prison of the believer." Higher than "this world" and "Paradise" is the "negation of individuality", negation of "I".

Abu Hasan served the poor, and he served in detachment. Have you seen a swimmer swimming in a river, striking the waters freely, without the impediment of clothes? So did Abu Hasan serve the poor – freely, without attachment, swimming in the *samsara* without the impediment of the outer, the external. He served and was not entangled in *moha* (attachment). He served the poor, and as they saw him, his tear-filled eyes, they were drawn to God, for they realised that Abu Hasan wept in longing for the Lord. And seeing him thus, they said. "He yearns for the Face of Allah, can he be denied the vision of His Face, the Purest of the pure, fair beyond compare?"

Jesus was asked which was the noblest, the purest and the best of all actions. And Jesus answered, "Love and longing for Him!" On another occasion, Jesus said: "If, indeed, when I enter into the innermost shrine of a dear one, I find there is no love of this world, nor love of Paradise, then am I filled with joy, and I fill him, My devotee, with love to Me, and I hold him fast and call him 'My friend'!"

Compassion filled the heart of Abu Hasan. He not only served men and animals, he blessed them all. He tended the wounded and nursed the sick; he spent lonely nights praying for the sorrowed ones.

According to a Muslim tradition, Abu Bakr once asked Muhammad for a prayer for private use, and the Prophet said, "Abu Bakr! Here is a prayer I give you. Pray it everyday:

> O Allah! God of Mercy!
> With sin have I wronged
> My own soul!
> Forgive me! For Thou alone
> Dost forgive all sins!
> Forgive me with Thy forgiveness,
> And have compassion on me–
> A sinner!
> For Thou art the Forgiver!
> And Thou art the Merciful!"

Abu Hasan meditated on *Al-Rehman*–God, the Merciful– and sang to Him again and again, sweetly, out of the fullness of his heart. He was well aware of the tragedy of sin, of cruelty of man to man, of poverty and starvation, of bloodshed and massacre, of impurity, slander and hate. But he believed profoundly in God's love and its power to make men new and rekindle in their hearts, the extinguished lamp again. Man, Abu Hasan thought of as a child, to whom a Light was given to guide him on the path of life. But man, Abu Hasan realised, was overtaken by storms again and again and the Light was extinguished, again and again. Yet, in the words of Farid, the mystic poet, was "the Light re-lighted once more and yet once more!"

Hasan speaks, again and again of the Beauty and Love of the Beloved. Of His Beauty are all the beauties of Nature reflected rays. Music and flowers are His reflections. Where, then, O Death! is thy sting? Abu Hasan gazes at Nature–the star-lit skies, the "brother sun, the sister water", the rose in the garden and the little bird nightingale – with joy in his heart.

This Muslim mystic worshipped God as the Lord of Life, he disowned Death! "I will not," he said, "give up my breath to Death. My breath is given me by the Lord of Life and to Him shall I surrender it!" And he left instructions that his tomb should be simple and not high. "Bury me," he said, "in a simple way, keep clear of shows. I need no more than a little space. Bayazid, the Blessed, was buried in a low, simple grave, let not my tomb rise higher!"

[4]

The richest treasure of a people or a race is the presence of truly spiritual men and the blessings which they diffuse.

Hasan poured blessings on all who met him. Rightly did they call him a *fakir*, as initiate, a seer of the Divine Secret. Hasan's life was centred in Allah. Allah is the Divine Principle of life.

He who invokes the Name of Allah, at once in his inward consciousness and his outer life, becomes a vehicle of God's grace. You may be prevented by illness or other outward circumstances from repeating your prayer, but nothing can prevent you from invoking the Name of Allah in your heart. This invocation is not an outer rite but an inward experience. We have a similar thought in a Hindu scripture, "There can be no doubt that a Brahmin will attain beatitude by *japa* (invocation of the Name) alone, whether or not he accomplishes other rites."

A *fakir* is never forgetful of the Name of Allah. Hasan was absorbed in the Name of Allah. Hasan was possessed by the Name, he was Name-possessed, God-possessed, God-intoxicated. His life was infused with the Holy Spirit.

The eye sees itself in the mirror. And in the mirror of Illumination, the mirror of the "Name", the the *fakir* sees his true Self. "Who speaks a better word," we read in the Muslim scripture, the Qur'an, "than he who calls on Allah? The Invocation of Allah is of all things the greatest." This invocation, indeed, polishes the heart, purifies it, and links it with the Holy Brotherhood of the Pure and Perfect Ones!

In Christian literature, we read of St. Bernard's converse with the Word of God, and of Brother Lawrence's "Practice of the Presence of God". And in the *Imitation of Christ*, we read of messages in the form of "distinct, interior words" received by him who is absorbed in "divine companionship". In these "discourses of the Divine Voice", we find that the language itself becomes sweet, lyrical, rich in rhythm and music. So, in lyrical, rhythmic language, Abu Hasan speaks of the dialogue between him and God. Abu Hasan says:

    Once I heard the Lord speak to me thus,
    "O thou, My servant and disciple!
    Dost thou feel unhappy and ask Me to give thee joy?
    Then shall I grant thee joy, indeed!

> Dost thou come to Me with a prayer to give thee wealth of the world?
> Then shall I grant thee the earth's treasures in abundance!
> Or dost thou come to Me in a spirit of self-surrender, saying, 'Lord! to Thee I surrender my I-ness, ego – all that I have?'
> Remember, I, too, shall say to thee,
> 'My child! thou hast renounced thy all to Me.
> I, too, shall renounce My all to thee!'"

In another passage, Abu Hasan writes:

> In my heart I heard
> One day the Voice of my Lord.
> The Voice said,
>   Abu Hasan!
>   Abide thou for ever
>   Obedient to My Will!
>   For know thou this
>   That I am the Ever-Loving One,
>   And Death cometh not
>   Nigh unto Me!
>   Be thou Mine
>   And I shall grant to thee
>   The strength to conquer Death!
>   So do thou refrain
>   From all things which I forbid.
>   I shall give thee
>   The Self-rule which shall not die!

In clear, emphatic terms he tells us in yet another passage:

> For thirty years have I spoken to the people. They think I tell them the things of my own. Alas! They forget that I speak to them of what is spoken to me.

On another occasion, he said:

> I heard in my heart a Voice say,
>   "Abu Hasan!
>   Everything shall I give unto thee,
>   But power and sovereignty shall never be thine!"

And I said,
> "My Master and my Lord!
> I need naught but Thee!
> Sovereignty and power give Thou to them
> Who are not knit together with Thee!"

Yes, Abu Hasan asked not for sovereignty and power. He rejoiced in poverty and renunciation.

He refers repeatedly to the converse between him and God in a hidden shrine within. It is the heart. Within is, also, the "lower" self, the "ego", the "I", the source of carnal desires. Yet, in the "hidden shrine of the Heart is the "Divine Spark", kindled when God breathed into man the Breath of His Spirit.

When desires came to dominate the life of man, he became impure, he came under the influence of *nafs* (I-self). "Blessed is the man," we read in the Revelation of Islam, "who hath kept his soul pure."

Suggestive symbols are used to indicate man's upward movement—ascent to the Life Divine. One of the symbols used is "pilgrim". As a pilgrim, he is a wanderer, filled with the longing to find his lost home.

Another symbol used is that of a lover filled with "craving of the heart" to meet his Beloved.

He begins to realise that he cannot see his Beloved until he has achieved inward purity. So in his journey to God, his pilgrimage, he learns (1) detachment, (2) humility, and (3) poverty of spirit or self-renouncement.

Achieving inward purity, he is transmuted. He becomes a new man. Through a process of self-stripping and utter renunciation, he attains to that stage in evolution which is called *fana* or annihilation:

> O, let me not exist!
> For non-existence proclaims
> In organ-tones,
> "To Him we shall return!"

[5]

In one of his "Sayings", Abu Hasan speaks of a "bazaar in the Road of Allah". In this bazaar, he tells us, there are pictures of beauty, pictures of the Other World, pictures of *tapasya* (self-control) pictures of meekness, pictures of the Heavenly Man. Blessed is he who goes to this bazaar and, standing there, gazes at the Pictures with longing in his eyes.

But he who would find the bazaar, enter therein, and gaze at the beauty of picture after picture, must (1) learn to renounce—must accept poverty and renounce the things of the earth and the ways of the world, (2) enter into silence, (3) in silence, meditate on the Lord, and (4) in meditation, enter the stream of Grace and, flowing in the stream, mingle at last with the Great Sea, forgetting the self, and become one with Him who is the One without a Second!

In the quest for Truth, the Divine Reality, an important step to take is poverty and love for the poor. A great Sufi rightly said, "If you are a true *dervish*, be kind to the poor. Behold! The disc of the sun gives the cloth of gold (sunlight) to the naked."

A mark of the Sufi's daily life was simplicity. "They are content," wrote an early interpreter of the Sufi Communities, "with little in the way of worldly goods, and are satisfied with simple diet: simple, too, are they in clothing and bedding. They choose poverty rather than riches. They renounce dignity, honour and rank, and in their heart is compassion to mankind and humility towards both the small and the great. They remain content even when God tries them and they endure with patience their continual struggles in opposition to the fleshly lusts, while they abstain from the pleasures of the carnal self and fight against it. They endeavour to realise that the carnal self is headstrong to do evil, and accept the teaching that the chief of a man's enemies is within himself."

Renunciation was the Sufis' joy. Abu Hasan's renunciation was not only of the "unlawful", but also of the "lawful", renunciation of all save God. Abu Hasan practiced fasting from time to time. He wished to eat only "lawful" food. "What is lawful?" they asked him. And he said, "That food is lawful which is earned by the labours of our own hands or which is earned by the honest means or which is provided by a few believers who love and fear God, and share their food with the poor." All food bought with money dishonestly earned was "unlawful."

Of Saint Ramakrishna, we read, that his hand in his attempt to take money – a source of unlawful things – would refuse to move! And of a Sufi who lived in accord with Abu Hasan's ideal, we read that his hand refused to move if he tried to stretch out his hand to take "unlawful" food.

Abu Hasan did not merely fast in Ramadan, he fasted also on other occasions also. His belief was that fasting was a help in mortifying the flesh and in gaining illumination of the heart. Abu Hasan believed and taught that fasting was a way to curb desire. The great Sufi thinker and theologian of Islam, Al-Ghazali, referred to some of the beautiful results of fasting in significant words thus:

1. Fasting helps in purification of the soul and illumination of the mind.
2. Fasting helps in learning humility.
3. Fasting awakens remembrance of the poor.
4. Fasting gradually breaks fetters to freedom from sinful desires.
5. Fasting is resistance to the temptation to sleep and a stimulus to remembrance of God.
6. Fasting helps us in building up our physical health.
7. Fasting reduces our expenses.
8. Fasting provides us, in some measure, with means to feed the poor.

More important than the fasting of the body, Abu Hasan taught, was the fasting of the heart, i.e. abstention from desire. More helpful, spiritually, than abstention from food is abstention from sinful desire. And when you save time by fasting, you give more time to prayer and to reading of the holy words written by holy men. So are you drawn nearer and nearer to God.

A Western mystic said, "Poverty is naught to have, and nothing to desire, but all things to possess in the spirit of liberty." Renunciation grows out of the thought on which we should do well to meditate, that what belongs to this world is transient and that only what belongs to God is abiding. Is not the abiding better than the transient? In the language of Al-Ghazali, "Jewels are better than snow. Snow exposed to the sun melts, but a precious stone never passes away."

True poverty is not merely of the material kind. In true poverty you are indifferent to both wealth and destitution. True poverty is inner.

So true renunciation is inner. In true renunciation, you break all connections with external objects, and you pass through life without attachment.

Abu Hasan was a lover, too, of silence. What is silence? Turning to God, said Abu Hasan.

In a well-known quotation from the *Qur'an*, the Voice says, "God will guide to Himself the one who turneth to Him." Turning to Him is turning to the Light. The Light of God, Abu Hasan taught, was veiled in many veils. "O Light of light! Thou art veiled to Thy creature and it does not attain to Thy Light." One by one, these "veils" will drop in the measure in which we try to commune with Him in silence. So Abu Hasan taught that we must keep away from the stress and strife, the talk and tumult of this earth-life. Abu Yazid said, "All the shout and strife of this earth is outside the Veil. Within the Veil is silence and calm and rest." Again, "Dost thou hear how there comes a Voice from the brooks of running water? But when they reach the sea, they are quiet!"

In silence you touch the realm of knowledge. And knowledge is not perfected until it attains annihilation. You truly know when you become a zero – a nothing! When you have nothing, are nothing, you are with the All! A great Sufi was once asked, "When does a man know that he has attained real knowledge?" He said, "At the time when he becomes annihilated – nothing!" When this blessed moment of self-annihilation arrives, you know.

Every day, therefore, Abu Hasan urges, men must be, for some time at least, alone with God. Not by means of thought but in and through silence may God be attained. When we enter more and more into silence, our desires are gradually eliminated, purity is attained, the body and the mind are sanctified, and we taste the Name Divine and know how sweet the Name is.

The organ of the Spirit, according to Abu Hasan, is the Heart. In silence is the Heart illumined. Veil after veil is removed in silence, and in the Heart shines the Light.

When the Light is seen shining within your heart, you behold the light in all that is outside you – the One Light in all. This is the Vision Universal – in which you see that the One is in all and that all are in the One! Abu Hasan says, "Blessed is he – the man of illumination! For wherever he be, he dwelleth with the One Eternal!"

Such a blessed one belongs not to this colour or caste or creed, he belongeth to all! The Illuminated Teacher, the great poet and mystic of Iran, Jalal ud-Din Rumi, rightly said:

> I am neither Christian nor Jew,
> Neither Gabir nor Turk.
> I am not of the East,
> I am not of the West.
> Nor of the Land,

Nor of the Sea
Am I!

I belong to the Soul of the Beloved!
I have seen that the two are one!
And One I seek,
And One I know!
One I see!
One I adore!

He is the First
And He is the Last!
He is the Outward
As he is the Inward, too!

[6]

Many from many towns and villages travelled to him, just to have a look at his face, to touch his lotus – feet and to receive his blessings.

One said to him, "Master! Give me a motto for meditation every morn."

And Abu Hasan said, "This be the motto I pass on to you– " 'Mine' and 'thine' both belong to Thee, O Lord!"

Asked, "What is service?", he said, "He that hath two garments, let him share with him who is naked. And let him not eat his food without sharing it with a hungry man or woman."

He freely gave food to the hungry. He often said, "The first lesson in the scripture of my life is – serve!"

"For years," he said, "have I cooked food, not for myself, but for the poor whom I call the guests of God. What I eat is the poor man's *prasad* (gift) to me."

"Give food to the poor," he said, "and compassion to the sinner and love to all creatures."

An influence went out of his words as he spoke to the young and the old. "How does he cast his spell over those who hear him?" they asked. "Who can say?"

And a disciple answered, "See him and hear him to understand. It is not merely the teaching of Abu Hasan, it is an *influence* moving out of him that captures you. It was but a week ago I heard him last. He was slender, but his eyes were bright. What did he say?

'Share the fruits of your work with the poor. Be not like the rich who prey upon the poor, paying them low wages.

'Be friends and brothers to all. A friend gives sympathy, but a brother bears burden in adversity.

'Let every house be a house of prayer, and let every man be a worshipper of God.

"Above all temples of brick and stone is the Temple of the Heart. Cleanse that temple."

Many more questions were put to him. Some of the these, with his answers, are indicated in brief thus:

Q: What is the supreme law of life?
A: Give thy life to Him and He will give His Life to thee, and free thee from the vanities of the world.

Q: How may I be perfect?
A: Annihilate thyself!

Q: What is the law of silence?
A: Be not talkative. And when you open your mouth, speak as far as possible of only God and of the Saints of God.

Q: How may I possess God for ever?
A: To live in the presence of a God-man is to see God and possess Him for ever!

Q: How may one vanquish the world?
A: If ye run after the world, the world will dominate you. Turn away from the world and you will transcend it.

Q: Who is a fakir of God?
A: One who is care-free and thinketh not of the morrow.

Q: What is the first step on the way to the true life?
A: The first step is *tauba*, repentance.

Q: What is the secret of repentance?
A: Turning away from all save God. Not remembrance of sins, but the forgetting of them. So, true repentance and *smaran* (God-remembrance) go together.

Q: Who is a true devotee of God?
A: He who never complains but accepts, all that comes from God—all benefits and all affliction.

Q: Has fear no place in spiritual life?
A: Yes, but only when fear is blended with love. And never forget that love of God perishes through pleasure and ease. Fear without love is slavish obedience.

Q: Who are they who put their trust in God?
A: They are the men who, in all situations, accept the will of God as, indeed, the best for them.

Q: Who are the poor in spirit?
A: They who lose themselves in the Infinite.

Q: Who are the inheritors of the legacy of saints?
A: Not they who are learned in the lore of books but they whose life is filled with the riches of renunciation. To them belongs the untold treasure of the saints.

Q: How may the soul, led astray by *nafs*, the carnal self, evil desires, be purified again?
A: The soul is purified by (1) faith in Allah, (2) recollection and repetition of the Divine Name.

[7]

He was a highly cultured man – a brilliant graduate of an Indian University. In the course of a talk on the challenge of modern thought and life, he asked me a significant question, "What is the meaning of history?"

In answer to it, I said, in brief, "The meaning of history is not to be found in the attainment of mere political freedom nor in the achievement of mere economic self-sufficiency. Material comfort and physical well-being have, indeed, a place in the programmes of life. But the centre of history is the *individual*. We are told the second indusrial revolution has begun! Yes, technology is making strides even in Eastern countries. Machinery and telephone and radio and television and aeroplane may help civilisation, but only in the measure in which they are God-guided."

Rightly asks Abu Hasan, "Where do I see God?"

"Where I do not see myself," is Hasan's answer.

My "self" is my "ego", "I", the sordid "self" of passion and pride. Out of this are the world's suffering and pain. "The whole world," says the *Gita*, "is entangled in activity." "Bitter art thou," says Hasan, "as long as thou art entangled in the world." Therefore is the world become – in spite of technology and education, inspite of scientific advance and industrial progress – a prison-house, and the nations groan beneath the burden of an aggressive civilisation, not knowing which way to go. "O brother!" cries Abu Haan, "When thou art released from the ego, from passion and pride and, being released, when thou taste and see how sweet is the Lord, then wilt thou attain a New Life of Freedom, Peace and Joy!"

"In the ego, in selfishness, in aggressiveness and hate," says this Sufi teacher, "does evil reside."

Hasan's "Sayings" are simple and luminous, radium-like. Their light appeared centuries ago: the light shines on. They have filled my heart with joy as I have reflected on them in silence:
> Be pure and God will pour on thee His love!
>
> *
>
> Desolate are they who leave this world without drinking of the nectar of the Wisdom of the Saints.
>
> *
>
> Which is the way to keep ever awake? This – to feel, as thou dost draw thy breath that it may be thy last!
>
> *
>
> Doth a dead body frighten thee? I am not afraid. Death cannot frighten one who is dead already!
>
> *
>
> None is my disciple. To none am I a *murshid*. I only know that the Lord alone sufficeth.
>
> *
>
> He who loveth not the little ones, how can he love the Lord?

*

Compared to this Wisdom, much of our modern "knowledge" is decadence. We, in this modern era, fight and make money, and fill our heads with shibboleths of science and politics. Hasan, in humility, was happy to withdraw within and discover the soul and surrender himself to its simplicities. In the modern era, the man with the highest heap is become our idol – an idol of clay! Hasan had that true culture whose heart turneth to God. It is the culture which makes the nations of East and West brothers and sisters in the One service of Life. Verily, this culture links us in love and sympathy with all creatures and with flowers and rivers and rains and the sun and the moon and the stars.

JUNNUNA MISRI

*"Meditation on God is my food,
His praise is my drink!"*

---

[1]

An interpreter of Christian thought spoke of Egypt as "the land of darkness". He spoke what history will reject as untrue. Egypt was, once, a centre of "schools of initiation", a home of "mysteries". Heraclitus and Pythagoras confessed that they had been initiated in Egypt into the "mysteries", and Neo-Platonism had its centre in Alexandria. In Egypt, there were groups of young men who studied the Nile and the heavens, and in Egypt were developed architecture, engineering, astronomy and astrology, at which we moderns may well marvel.

Cairo was the richest city west of the Indus: Cairo was the homeland of medieval music in Islam: Cairo was a shrine of art and culture. In this land of a thousand lutes, we have, at this very hour, the oldest existing University–the University of el-Azhar. It is an international University, drawing pupils from all the Muslim world–from Persia to Zanzibar from China and Japan. A remarkable University! Students pay no fees: teachers receive no pay.

Today, el-Azhar has some ten thousand students and three hundred professors. And it is an impressive sight to see groups of students in the cloisters of a mosque – a thousand year old mosque – each group squatting in a semicircle before a revered teacher. Impressive, too, is the great Hall of Wisdom in the University. In this great University, God is, to students and professors, a reality, not an abstraction. Five times a day, they bend themselves in reverence before God. Their faith in a Higher Power has much to teach the modern man.

And their reverence for the Prophet Muhammad, is profound. Was he not a man of deep humility and prayer? He claimed no more than that he had a "message for mankind". "I am one like unto you—a man," he said. And on the day he was leaving the world for his Unseen Home, he said to them, "Do not rush at one another's throat after I go, for, one day, you will have to face Allah, who will require you to answer for your sins."

And Egypt was, for some time, a spiritual teacher of Greece and Rome. Egypt became a homeland of friars and fakirs. In Egypt lived, in the Muslim era (when Khalifas ruled Baghdad), a great teacher of spiritual science, a Master of wisdom. They called him Misri (Egyptian)—more fully, "Junnuna Misri". He rose to a vision of the Truth that is universal. The Truth that discards neither Muslim nor Hindu, neither Christian nor Buddhist, neither Greek nor Jew, but embraces them all in a unity that the sages of India have adored as the *Ekameva dvityam*—the One without a second. Pure pearls—gems of the purest ray serene—have I found in the words of this "Egyptian Master". And I have marvelled at the man and his depth of perception and significance. He says:

> Common is the sight of men who bear misfortune, but how uncommon the sight of the blessed ones who bear the buffets of fate, yet do not lose the peace of the soul!

*

> If thou has met God, He is enough—the One True Friend in life. If thou hast not met Him, meet them who are His friends and thou wilt be happy.

*

Thou cravest for company? Then be in the company of those who have risen above the distinctions of "I" and "Thou". Theirs are consecrated lives!

*

Never think of any creature as mean. Never think of anyone as inferior to thee. Open the inner eye that beholdeth the Countenance of God and thou wilt see that in all creatures shineth the One Glory!

*

Meditation on God is my food, His praise is my drink, and to bear witness to His glory is my garment.

*

On these and many other Sayings of this Teacher have I meditated, from time to time, and have found them charged with the wisdom of the *Gita* and the teaching of the *Upanishads*. In the thought of this Egyptian Master, I find a psychology which sees the vanity of logic and argumentation, an ethic which sees the God beyond all gods–the illusory appearances of the surface we call the world–and a philosophy which sees that deeper than science or politics or industry is the meditation which reveals the depth of life concealed from those who live as captives in the heavy chains of desire.

[2]

God works in strange ways His wonders to perform. In a strange way was Junnuna's life transformed. The transformation is nothing short of a revolution. He is young. He hears, again and again, of a holy man. Junnuna goes to meet this man of God, this *tapasvin* (ascetic). Junnuna finds the *tapasvin* is suspended in a tree, his head downwards his feet upwards and he is repeatedly saying to himself, "O thou, my body! If thou wilt not cooperate with me in my spiritual aspirations and discipline, I shall torture thee thus! I shall keep thee hungry and thirsty until thou diest!"

Junnuna weeps as he hears these words. The *tapasvin* hears the sobs of Junnuna and, calling him, says, "Look, who is there who will have compassion upon one who is not only full of sins but is not ashamed of sins?"

Junnuna asks, "I understand you not. Tell me clearly what you mean."

The *tapasvim* says, "Look! This body of mine refuses to help me in the service and worship of the Lord. This body would rather mix with the crowds and make merry. So I am teaching it the practice of abstinence."

Junnuna asks, "Have you committed murder or some other heinous sins?"

"No!" said the *tapasvin*.

"Are you a great *vairagi* (ascetic)?" asked Junnuna.

"No! No!" exclaimed the *tapasvin*. "If you would see a great *vairagi*, ascend this mountain and see him on the top!"

Junnuna goes up the mountain and sees that at the door of a cottage was sitting a *tapasvi*, His one foot is inside the cottage: his other foot, which is cut, is outside the cottage: ants have surrounded it. Junnuna draws near, salutes him, and asks what the matter is.

The *tapasvi* says, "I sat in my cottage one day, and I saw in front of me a young woman coming out of her house. I saw her and was bewitched with her beauty. I longed to see her lovely face again. So I stood up and hardly had I put my foot outside my cottage, when I heard suddenly a voice saying to me, 'O ascetic! Art thou not ashamed of thyself? Thou hast glorified the Lord for thirty years. Thou dost call thyself a *bhakta* (devotee of the Lord) yet art thou entangled in the snare of Satan! Beware! Rise above the glamour ! Awake! Or be thou fallen in the pit of hell!'

"And listening to these words, I trembled. I cut the foot which I had placed outside the cottage. I threw the foot outside. Since then I have sat here, patiently awaiting what is to come. Brother! Why hast thou come to me, a sinner? If thou wouldst see a true *Mahatma* (saint), then go forward, Thou wilt see him on yon mountain-height!"

Junnuna is unable to ascend so high. So he returns to the *tapasvi* and enquires of him all about the *Mahatma*. The *tapasvi* says, "On yon mountain heights sits a true *sadhu*, a *Mahatma*. One day, there came to him a man, who said, 'If a man will not earn, how will he live? Life depends on your daily exertions. What can the grace of God do, unaided by human efforts?' Hearing this, the *Mahatma* said to himself, 'Is not the grace of God all-sufficient? If a man will not work hard, does God become impotent to help him? I resolve not to eat what a man may bring to me.' And for several days the *tapasvi* ate nothing. Then God guarded his life—how? The bees came and built a home there, and the honey of that home was eaten by the *tapasvi*. His life was saved!"

Junnuna hears this and his heart is filled with faith in God and God's unfailing love. "He will take care of me," says Junnuna. "He will not leave me in the dust."

Junnuna returns home. On the way, he saw a blind bird alighting from a tree. And says to himself, "Whence does this blind bird get his daily food?"

What does Junnuna see? The blind bird scratches the earth and underneath are a few grains and drops of water. The bird eats and drinks, and is perched again upon the tree. Junnuna's faith in God is intensified. Junnuna's life is revolutionised. He becomes new!

Not yet is he become a Master, but he has received his first lesson. He now longs to live a New Life. He longs to be desireless. He begins to see the world of life in the light of God – the Providence of all! He sees that in him started the process of a new creative life. New aspiration takes birth within him. He begins to see the vanity of earthly ambitions, of honours and fame. He grows in the strength to renounce!

[3]

He is not yet pure enough. "God, the great Master," he says, "will purify me and, in His good time, make me a child of His Light—a child of Grace—and, passing through the fire, I too, may shine as gold thrice-refined!"

Junnuna prays intensely, "O Lord! Make me Thine. Let not the world overwhelm me! But fill me with Thy presence that I may see Thy beauty everywhere!"

One day, he goes to a river to have his bath and offers his prayers to God. He enters into the river, when lo and behold, his eyes are turned to the roof of a radiant house. One was standing on the rooftop and Junnuna's eyes are there— transfixed! He is absorbed in a form of wondrous beauty. A young woman is standing on the roof, and Junnuna looks on! Junnuna has lost himself in this vision of loveliness. And, waking from this vision, he says to her, "O beautiful one! Are you married? And what is your name?"

And she answers, "Junnuna! You are no stranger to me. Your name has travelled to me, and I was told that you were a *fakir*, a man of realisation, wisdom-filled, God-intoxicated. And when I saw you at a distance, I was filled with a longing to see you from near and be blessed. Now I see you near and now I know. Alas! That earthly beauty bereaves you of reason and self-control!"

Longing to hear her more—for to him her words were sweeter than honey—he says, "Speak to me more clearly, for my mind is confused. And true it is, I feel, at this moment, like a drunken man!"

And she, in whose heart is love of God and love of the Saints of God, speaketh, her eyes radiant with compassion and humility, "Junnuna! If you were a *fakir*, you would not be distracted by a form. If you were a man of realisation, you would know that what endureth not, is, for ever and ever, only a dream. If you were wisdom-filled, your heart would rise above desire and be lifted to the beatific vision of eternal Truth. If you were God-intoxicated, your joy would be in Him, not in a frail, fickle creature of dust and desire—in Him and His Light, which is brighter than the sun, the moon and the stars!"

So saying, she vanishes. And Junnuna turns this way and that. She hath vanished and tears tremble in his eyes. And for some moments, he meditates upon her words and says to himself, "What she hath said of me is true. Every word of that radiant one had a ring of sincerity. It is true, I am not yet become a true *fakir*. Wisdom is still afar! For I see, that in my heart is a flame, not a spring of the holy water that heals, and in mine eyes is still earthly desire, not the intoxication of the Eternal Name. What right have I to live? Death! O Death! Come and enfold me!"

[4]

Junnuna now enters into the waters of the Nile. He wishes to drown himself. The Nile is like the Indus – a river rapid but erratic.

A merchant's boat is moving on the waters. Someone in the boat sees Junnuna drowning and raises cry. Save, O save! The boat stops and picks up Junnuna. He is saved, and he is beaten – blow after blow falling upon his back and his face. The merchant strikes him, beats him black and blue. Why? The merchant has lost precious pearls and suspects Junnuna to be the thief! But Junnuna bears all the blows with the patience of a true *bhakta*. Junnuna says to himself, "O Lord! Thou knowest all!"

The lost pearls are later, found elsewhere and the merchant, on bended knee, tells Junnuna, "Forgive me! I have beaten you and I have sinned!"

Junnuna forgets what has happened–never forgets the mercy of the Lord. "Yea, though I walk through the valley of death, I will fear no evil, for Thou art with me. Thy rod and Thy staff–they shall comfort me." The Lord hath saved Junnuna, the Lord hath punished him! He feels purified and sheds tears in longing for the Lord. And he is out, again, in quest!

[5]

One day, as he goes up a mountain, he sees a number of men and women. They are all sick and afflicted. They have congregated in one place.

He asks, "Why are so many come together in this place on mountain heights? And they all are sick and afflicted!"

One of them says, "In yon cottage dwells a *tapasvi*, a holy man. Once a year he cometh out of his cottage and, with his healing breath, he heals the sick and then enters again the cottage. Today is the annual day of pilgrimage to him, and so the crowds are come together here to see him and be healed."

After some time, this holy man cometh out of his cottage. His body was so frail – bones without flesh and blood. Pallor is on his lips, his eyes are sunk in their sockets, but his face is radiant with a strange, unearthly light. And, as he comes out, he gazes with compassionate eyes on the men and women who are come to see him and be cured. Then, he lifts his eyes in supplication to the Heavens above. Then, he calls each patient to himself, and into each he breathes the breath of his benediction. He heals them, then goes to his cottage. And as he goes, Junnuna clings to his feet and says, "O holy one! Thou hast cured so many. Look thou on me, too, with eyes of compassion, for I, too, suffer. In the Name of Allah (God) I ask thee to heal me!"

The healer hears Junnuna and says, "Junnuna, leave me! I am nothing. On the high throne sitteth He, who seeth all – my Beloved, your Friend! Go to Him! Take shelter at His feet! He will heal you!"

And the holy man reenteres his cottage. And Junnuna learns to enter into the cave of his heart. There he seeks the Lord, until he finds Him. For ever the Lord seeketh His own. He finds us first, then are we God-possessed, absorbed in the Eternal.

[6]

Junnuna now attracts some – seekers of God. They come from towns and villages. They sit at his feet to learn from him the truths of spiritual life. They take his name afar, and in Egypt, Arabia and Turkestan they call him the "Egyptian Master". But they are not many.

What a mercy of God when a great Teacher appears! Democracy makes a mistake in supposing that a crowd can understand and choose. Crowds lack comprehension. A Master is understood only by prepared souls. And many do not understand the Master. They called him a *Kafir* (infidel). The *mullahs* (Muslim priests) hate him as a heretic.

They carry reports to the Khalifa of Baghdad. Egypt was, in those days, a province of this Khalifa: and he is poisoned against the Master. Junnuna is seized and brought to Baghdad. In silence, stands he before the Khalifa. So Jesus stood before Pilate. Junnuna speaks not a word, but his eyes were aglow with a great Light. His silence is eloquent.

An old man draws nigh to him and whispers to him, "Your eyes and your silence bear witness to your wisdom. You are not a culprit. You are a servant of God, a messenger of His Truth. And without His Will no one can touch a hair on your head. Mind not the *mullahs*. If it be God's will that you go to prison, in prison, we know, you will glorify Him!"

And Junnuna is sent to jail! Again and again, have the messengers of God been imprisoned, persecuted, crucified or shot to death. But Truth is not stifled. Truth shines radiant on the gallows and in jail.

Junnuna goes to jail with a smile on his lips. The sun is still upon the hilltops. A few of the Master's disciples are with him at the jail gate. Their tears are flowing fast. "Weep not," he says to them, "I wish to go in peace. And naught happens without the Will of Allah. In Him is our peace!"

One of the wisest, the purest and the best of men goes into jail, unmourned, except by a few. The majority are under the influence of the *mullahs*. They call him an atheist! And this atheist taught that there is but one God, and in Allah, the Eternal, is the peace of man! The majority fail to understand the Master. Men in crowds are swayed by harangues, not thought. Plato urges that numbers are no index to wisdom, and that crowds are ruled by demagogues, "who go ringing on in long harangues, like brazen pots, which, when struck, continue to sound till a hand is put upon them!" A society is in peril when led by its demagogues, not its purest and wisest men.

Junnuna is in jail for forty days. Hunger enfeebles him, but he is steadfast in fast and prayer. On being released, he walks, but he was so weak that he falls, again and again, on the ground. His head bleeds.

In this state, he is brought before the Khalifa. The news spreads quickly abroad. His disciples gather in the garden of the Khalifa's mansion. They see the Master again, but are filled with indignation when they see him tired, exhausted, worn out, with blood-marks on his head.

Junnuna stands before the Khalifa in the garden: and the courtiers are around the Khalifa. The Khalifa looks at Junnuna and is moved by what he sees – a Teacher dear to his disciples as the Master, in tattered clothes, blood-stained, yet with eyes glowing with a strange, mystic light. The Khalifa offers Junnuna a seat and asks him to sit down. Then follows a little talk between the two.

Khalifa: "Junnuna! You are now free. But see that you teach nothing subversive of the state or the social order."

Junnuna: "I teach as I have been taught."

Khalifa: "What have you been taught?"

Junnuna: "This, O ruler of men, that if a society would have life, it must live by the law of love, and that if a state would be strong, it must be ruled by guardians of the moral law and they must live a simple, frugal life—as lived the early Khalifas. They lived a hard and simple life. They eschewed luxury. They revealed Allah, the Eternal, in daily life. Their aspiration was not long prayers but communion with the Divine in silence and alms to the poor. They were the friends and guardians of the people. They were the sons of Light!"

As Junnuna speaks, the Khalifa listens and quietly drinks in the words, one by one. And as Junnuna closes his little but lyrical talk, the Khalifa bursts into tears. And the courtiers and disciples, too, weep. There is, for a few minutes, a hush of holy silence. Then the Khalifa falls at Junnuna's feet and says, "Master, forgive me. Accept me as thy disciple!"

A miracle has happened! Such miracles have happened again and again, in the history of the God-men, the mystics of Illumination, the sons of Light! The Khalifa now requests the Master to stay in the palace. The Khalifa serves the Master with wonderful devotion. Junnuna had no thought of founding a sect. His gentle life influences many, and his teaching regarding Allah, the Eternal, travels to several towns and villages. He teaches that Allah, the Eternal, is the Light of the dawn and the setting sun, is the Beauty of the blue sky and the Breath of the living air, is the Wisdom of the pure in heart and the Radiance of the life of His lovers and saints.

For some time he stays in the palace, then takes leave of the Khalifa and returns to Egypt.

[7]

Bank to his homeland – at last! Junnuna is out of his seclusion to give his message to multitudes. He thrills them. They call him Junnuna Misri. They revere him as a Master of Wisdom. And crowds are moved by his "Sayings." Here are a few:

> When the Lord showers His love upon His servants, He becomes their Eyes, their Ears, their Hands. Then through Him they see, they hear, they speak, they give and take!
>
> *
>
> Listen not to them who praise thee for gifts or charity or good deeds. The praise is not thine: the praise is His who giveth all!
>
> *
>
> First be a servant of God. And until thou art become His servant, do not say thou art Divine: else wouldst thou go into the deepest darkness of Hell!
>
> *
>
> Two marks there be of him who is a true lover of the Lord: (1) he is stable in censure and praise: and (2) he does his duty without a desire for fruit.
>
> *
>
> Be not attached to them who are to the world attached. Do not flatter them who give money or gifts. And hate no man who causeth thee harm!
>
> *
>
> Many find a solace in these wonderful words. Are they not full of assurance, illumination and inspiration?
>
> *

[8]

Junnuna spends the eve of his life in Egypt. The Egyptian Master's name travels, far and wide. His influence grows. His life fascinates many: they meditate on the grandeur of his sufferings and the glory of his teaching. The *Mullahs* continue to call him an infidel, and atheist: but he has lighted a fire which not all their efforts can quench. Fate has written that Junnuna should belong to all. From province to province, spreads the message of this man who has searched and found, has wandered and suffered and, at last, attained! In his heart there is room for all – the Sunni and the Shiah, the Jew and the Christian, the Greek and the Gentile. And to all men in his quiet, gentle way, he points the Way of Blessedness.

Junnuna is become a servant of Allah. And He hath looked upon His servant with love. And out of the mouth of Junnuna speaketh Allah, and out of the eyes of His servant looketh the Lord.

"What is your food?" they ask Junnuna.

And he answers: "Communion with God is the daily food of my life!"

"Why are you so patient with your opponents?" they ask him.

And he answers: "Truth is the Sword of God, and it never fails!"

"Who is the true giver of alms?" he is asked.

And in answer he says: "The true giver is he who never opens his ears to hear his praise. The true giver understands that all praise is the Lord's and that unto Him is all glory!"

"Is not man divine?" they ask him.

And he says: "Yes; but the proof that a man is divine is this, that he is ever-increasingly a servant of Allah, the Eternal!"

"And what are the sings of a true servant?"

Junnuna says: "Two signs. (1) He suffers: and (2) in the midst of all sufferings he keeps his mind unuffled. He lives in the presence of Great Peace."

Three of the rules of spiritual life he gives to his disciples, impress me much. These are: (1) keep away from men addicted to this world; (2) never flatter the rich nor those who give in charity; and (3) never hate those who harm you.

"What is the secret of the dedicated life?" he is asked. And he says, "The secret lies in self-forgetfulness. Forget yourself, forget your work, and see that your hope is in God alone, in none else, in none else!"

And this, too, he says, "The world is whatever keeps you away from God! And he is a low-caste man who walketh not the way that leadeth unto the Lord!"

A disciple asked him, "Master! Whose company may I keep?"

And the Master says, "His who has no sense of 'thine' and 'mine'!"

In a discourse, the Master says, "Regard not the creatures as mean or inferior to you. Open the Inward Eye, and you will behold the glory of Allah, the Eternal—in all!"

Speaking to a man who had spent years in sin, he says, "Let not your past sit as a burden upon you! Think of the Present and the God of the Present. In Him, be absorbed and sing His Name!"

"Who is the happy man?" asks a disciple.

And the Master says, "He who knows God and is in Him absorbed!"

Speaking of the "Steps of Ascent", the Master says, "He who would ascend to Allah, the Eternal, must mount up the following steps: (1) giving up running after the things of the world; (2) aversion for worldly pleasure; (3) purity; and (4) each day, growing in the love of God!"

In these Sayings of the Master is a treasure of infinite value, which will never perish. Surely, these are not the

"Sayings" of an "impious atheist", but of a singular man, God-absorbed and dedicated to the Life Divine!

[9]

One day, he was crossing a field: he finds it covered with snow. A man is near: he is throwing grains on the ground.

The Master asks "Brother! The ground is covered with snow. Why do you throw the grains on the ground?"

The man answers, "Yes, today the ground is covered with snow, and the birds know not where to go for food. For them I throw these grains on the ground, that they may eat them when they can. The Lord will accept these little grains which I offer in devotion to the little birds."

Soon after, the Master goes to Mecca and he sees the very man there as a devotee of God, going around the Kaaba. Seeing Junnuna, this man says, "How are you? You see how Allah has accepted my humble, little service to the birds! I threw the grains on the ground. See the 'fruit' now! God has had mercy on me and brought me to this holy place."

"Yes," says Junnuna, "the Lord accepts every little grain offered to His creatures with devotion!"

So Sri Krishna says to Arjuna in the *Gita*, "A leaf, a flower, a fruit, a little water—I accept every little gift offered with devotion."

[10]

Beautiful was the Master's life. Beautiful, too, was his death! Serene, he lies on his death-bed.

A disciple asks him, "Master! Tell us what is your desire at this moment."

The Master says, "This only, that He be near me as I am nearing death, so that He – my Friend – may enter again into my song and reveal again His radiant Face to me!"

So saying, the Master sings a song in Arabic – a song filled with singular love and longing for Allah, the Eternal.

Then comes his last utterance before he passes on to his Abode, "I am absorbed in the grace and love of my Beloved – of Allah, the Eternal."

Junnuna lived God-absorbed. And God-absorbed, his soul ascended to the Home of Glory. The sun shone in splendour at that time: and, as in the case of St. Francis – a lover of God and God's creatures – so in the case of Junnuna – a lover of God and the little birds of God – group after group of birds came and fluttered over him and received his blessings in the hour of his death.

*

His thoughts were deeper than the sea, and in his life was a beauty brighter than the beauty of the moon and the stars. In the years to be, pilgrims from India to Egypt will come to the spot where Junnuna breathed the last benediction of his earth-life, bow in lowly reverence to his blessed name and say, "Here was one, who taught that wisdom, not wealth, is the Way – one who saw the face of God unveiled, as did Kasyapa and Agastya, Yagnavalkya and Brihaspati, and other holy Rishis of India, in the long, long ago!"

SACHAL SARMAST

"Behold within thyself the Wonder!"

[1]

On the fourteenth of Ramzan, in 1829 A.D., he left this world. And every year, that day, a *mela* (gathering) is held at Darazan – the village which is become a shrine to many – where he passed away. In thousands they come there, every year, to get blessings of Sachal who, they say, is not dead but has only departed and who has greater power now to bless and heal the heart.

Today, Sind, a part of Pakistan, is under influences which appreciate Iqbal more than the Sufi poets and seers of Sind. At one time, indeed, while the Kalhoras – descended from a holy *fakir* – and the Talpurs – offspring of simple shepherds – ruled, the rustic people of Sind rejoiced in their singers and saints.

The genius of Sindhi poetry is, essentially, lyrical. In Sachal and Shah Latif, in Bedil and Sa'mi, the lyrical is blended—as in Jalal ud-Din Rumi and Jami of Iran—with the mystical and meditative. Sachal's lyrics aspire to a living and loving union with the One who transcends the many that change and pass. The "many" are the veils which shut out the Light. They must be pierced through to behold the Adorable Face of the Beloved.

Today, Sind needs must study anew Shah Latif, Sa'mi, Sachal and other Sufi poets. They purify the heart and the affections, while current education makes us clever, controversial, communal and sectarian. When will new schools appear? When will Sind be born anew?

The very heart of true mysticism is expressed in the following song of Sachal:

> The Beloved is within thee!
> Go and search! You will find
> The Beloved in the heart within!

Sachal was a true *fakir* of God. Who is a *fakir*? The word in Arabic, means "poor". "Blessed are the poor in spirit," said Jesus. Was not Jesus a *fakir*, too? Did he not say to his disciples, "Call me, 'O poor one!' "I have nothing by day and nothing by night. Yet I am the richest among the sons of men!"

So, Sachal, having no worldly possessions, loved to think of himself as a "king among men". "You see me," he said, "in a *fakir's* garb. But if you will know my inner self, you will know that I am not a beggar, but a king amongst men."

I love to think of Sachal as belonging to the "Brotherhood of the saints of God". "Jesus," said a great Sufi, "is the seal of the saints." Sachal was at once a poet and a saint. Entire self-surrender to God is the secret of a true saint. Therefore, is he, a man of purity, humility and meekness. Sachal was a true saint, a true *fakir*. Such an one hath three marks.

The first is devotion to the Name of God. A true *fakir* is he who sings the Name. With what joy did Sachal sing the Name! In his eyes was radiant the light of the Name. In his sleep, his dreams and daily activities, in the aspirations and illuminations of his heart, he sang the One Name Divine.

Another mark of a true *fakir* is meditation.

Yet another mark, too, has a saint. He combats and conquers passion, appetite. He knows there is, in the world, a *divya shakti*, a Divine Energy, a Spiritual Force called God. But there is, also, a Dark Power – passion. He battles with it and conquers it. He conquers because he has the "strength of ten", through communion with the *murshid* – the Teacher – and the Holy Spirit in the heart.

Sachal sang many of his poems in the name of "Khudai". The meaning of the word is the "Divine Life." The center of this life – the Life Divine – is the Heart. The Holy Spirit dwells in the Heart of man. The word used by Sachal and other Sufi singers and thinkers is *qalb*. It is of two kinds. There is the *qalb* the heart, which is the centre of earthly appetites, and there is the *qalb* the Heart, which is pure and divine – the throne of God. It is the Heart *haqiki*. It is the shrine of Eternal Beauty – the shrine of the Beloved. Sachal referred to this Heart, in words charged with deep yearning, in the following poem:

> To my courtyard He came.
> Blessed, blessed am I!
> He came to my courtyard–He!
> In love was my heart knit to Him.
> He came to meet me, a poor fakir!
> Messengers did I send Him, again and again,
> With the one message,
> "When wilt Thou come? When?"
> At last, He came.
> To my courtyard He came.
> He came to knit this poor fakir
> To His Feet divine!
> He came to take me Himself
> To the Realm where shines the Light
> Of the Ancient, Eternal One!

Sach al was, also, called *sarmast* (God-intoxicated). He lived and sang as an inspired man.

They called him masta (intoxicated). Sachal would sing of God the Beloved, and enter, again and again, into the superconscious. His companions called it *masti* or madness. This, the great seer, Plotinus, called ecstasy. Sachal would sing, *tambura* (one stringed instrument) in his hand, then would dance in divine enthusiasm until he passed into ecstasy.

Sachal was a love-intoxicated seer and singer of the God. Every inch of this man was charged with love. There are passages in Sachal's songs which remind me of the teaching of Father Zossima–the most spiritual character, perhaps, of Dostoevsky. In one of the scenes depicted by the great Russian writer, Father Zossima kneels down, kisses the ground before a sinner – a sacrilegious libertine – and, intoxicated with love, says:

> Love all God's creation–every grain of sand and every leaf and every ray of God!
> Love animals! Love plants! Love everything!
> Love everything and you will arrive at God's Secret of things!

So great was Sachal's love for all and so deep his humility that he never called anyone his disciple. He felt happy to find that Hindus and Muslims came and sat together in the "Fellowship Meetings". "Blessed," he would say, "blessed is he who listens to the *Bani*–the Word of Inspiration."

Sachal's great contemporary Bedil – singer and poet, refers to Sachal as a "symbol of Love Divine", a "God-intoxicated" man. "In Sachal's words," Bedil adds, "was a flame of the Eternal. In his ecstasy and inspiration, he resembled Attar, the ever-blessed. Sachal was of the great army of Lovers of the Light!"

In a beautiful, little poem, Sachal says:

> I went to the bazaar, one day.
> I saw a bulbul (nightingale) in children's hands.
> With a red string, they tied the bulbul tight.
> I went to the bulbul and said,
> "O song-bird of plaintive love!
> Why didst thou leave the fair garden
> For this place of imprisonment?"

The bulbul smiled and said,
"Dost thou not know
That he who would walk the way of love,
Must wear the cordon red
And sacrifice his all to the Beloved?"

In this two-fold note of sacrificial love and self-reverence, is Sachal's key to the dedicated life. Sachal says:

Renounce all doubts concerning thyself:
Realise the unity with the Eternal!
Behold within thyself the Wonder!
Why dost thou wander far and wide?
Dost thou seek the Beloved? Then know
The Beloved is in the shrine of the Heart within!

[2]

Sachal was born in the year 1739 A.D., in a quiet, little village in Sind. The village is known as Darazan. Darazan belongs to Khairpur, a state ruled by a Mir. In Darazan stands a monument to Sachal, built by a disciple – the Ruler, in those days, of Khairpur – and repaired, some years ago, by Sachal's successor – Sakhi Qabbol Muhammad.

Abdul Wahab was Sachal's name, he loved to be called "Sachedino". The meaning of the word is, "a gift from the Ture one", "a gift from God who is Truth". Sachal was, verily, God's gift to Humanity, God's gift to the people of Sind. In many of his poems, he calls himself "Sachoo". And it is true he spoke the truth not minding what others said.

A beautiful story is told of Sachal's boyhood. He was hardly seven years of age, when the great Poet-Saint of Sind, Shah Latif, comes to Darazan on a visit to Sachal's grandfather, Sain Morago. Shah Latif sees Sachal, blesses him and says, "You are destined, my child, to unveil the secrets of the Wisdom these lips have declared to the people. Blessed are you!" Sachal proved, indeed, to be a revealer and an interpreter of the Wisdom of spiritual life.

Sachal was a child when his father died. Sachal thereafter, lived with his uncle, Pir Abdul Haq. He was a pious man. Sachal regarded him as his *murshid* (Teacher). Sachal says in a little poem, "My Teacher was Abdul Haq. He was not a slave-soul but a free soul, whose life was filled with love for *Haq* or the Truth." Pure was he and truthful in speech and action. His wife was alive for two years only: he did not marry again. Sachal, as a child, was looked after by a nurse, whom Abdul Haq always treated with high regard. She was a pious woman. Sachal called her "mother". Blessed was she!

Abdul Haq was influenced by an order of the Fakirs, named the Chishti Order – a Sufi Order, of which the first center in India was Lahore. From Lahore, the Chishti Order advanced first to Delhi and then to Ajmer. The Chishti Order put emphasis on purity of the heart and spoke of the spiritual value of music.

The Sufi leader of this Order, in the twelfth century, was Khwaja Mulinuddin Chishti. The Khwaja was a remarkable man. They called him the "spiritual king of Muslim India" (*Sultan-i-Hind*). He was born in Seistan. He travelled widely in Isalmic countries. He was a wandering hermit. He was nearing fifty when he came to India. He chose to settle down in Ajmer where the Hindus were conservative in their outlook of life. Ajmer was then ruled by Rai Prithvi Raj. The priests asked the Raja to banish the Khwaja. His influence had travelled to the "lower classes" of Ajmer. The Raja sent an order of expulsion through Ram Deo, the head of the Hindu priests. Ram Deo proceeded to serve the order personally on the Khwaja. But on seeing the Khwaja, Ram Deo was so deeply impressed that he became a disciple and spent the years of his life in the service of the "lower classes", whom Hindu society, alas, did not treat in accordance with the teaching of India's *rishis* and saints.

One of the holy men of this Order, in Sachal's days, was Fakir Muhakam al-Din. Abdul Haq knew the holy *fakir* and dropped a letter to Sachal, saying, "The holy fakir is traveling to Sind and will be crossing the valley. Please go and meet him on my behalf and greet him with your hands on his feet and give him my salutations of love and serve him as best you can."

Sachal proceeded without delay to pay his respects to the holy *fakir* and found him seated on a weak horse. The *fakir* met Sachal cordially, saying, "Welcome, my child! Take this from me as a gift of my love to you!"

The *fakir* moved an arrow over Sachal's heart, and then, moved on! It was an arrow whose influence went into Sachal's heart, and Sachal was wounded with sympathy and love for the creation of God that groaneth in suffering and pain.

At the feet of his uncle, Sachal had his early lessons in education. Abdul Haq taught Sachal that true education was of the Heart. Sachal assimilated the truth that the gift most acceptable to God was the gift of the Heart. "O rich man! If thou bring God a hundred sacks of gold, He will say to thee, 'Bring thy Heart as a gift to My Door!'" He who gathers silver and gold becomes old, but he is ever young, whose name is writ or sung—in flower or stream or shining star, or in the dreams of beauty and truth!

Sachal's heart was enriched in solitude and loneliness. He would often close the door and be alone with Allah, the Eternal. He would close the door and have converse with God. To Sachal, as to al-Ghazali, came the realisation that a true Sufi was a man of intuition and meditation, not of words. Sachal rejoiced in communion with God. "He only knoweth God, to whom God hath shown Himself!" Again and again,

Sachal fell into deep "unconsciousness" and there came to him, the realisation that Truth was, verily, known in ecstasy.

Sachal's eyes were often wet. Night after night, he kept awake to converse with God. His face was radiant with beauty. When he opened his lips and sang of love and the Beloved, his long, flowing hair often standing erect, he won many hearts to the Life Divine.

Simple was Sachal–in dress, in diet, in daily life. He wore in winter and summer, coarse *khadi* cloth and said, "I am happy, very happy!" From wine and opium and other intoxicants, he kept aloof. His one intoxication was the Name of the Eternal–Allah. In one of his poems, Sachal sings:

> The Murshid (Teacher) spake
> To me, one day, thus,
> "Renounce thy friendship with the world,
> Remember the One Only Name,
> And forget everything else!"

In the desert, he spent much time in silence. In the desert, he listened to the still, small voice within. In the stillness of the desert he sat, communing with the Mystery that is God.

A few came, sometimes, to sit with him in meditation. "Where two or three are gathered in My Name, there am I, in the midst of them." He would often sit by a window, looking out of it and, again and again, would go into a deeper silence on beholding a form of the Beauty, such as that was not seen on earth or sea.

He was a lover of the Beautiful. Beauty was, to him, a theophany – a manifestation, an "emanation" of the Eternal Face. "In every form," he said, "behold the One Face of Beauty. To see aught else is a sin!"

Sachal loved to adore God as *Haq –Truth*. Haq, truth, Sachal said, was a Hidden Treasure. The Hidden Treasure,

God made manifest in the "mirror" of *maya*, and creation came into being. In a poem, Sachal says:

> He, the Friend, came
> To the Bazaar of Egypt.
> He came to offer Himself–
> His Beauty supernal.
> He came to see Himself–
> The King of Beauty!

Sachal worshipped God as Truth and Beauty. "Follow the Truth," Sachal said. He did not follow opinion, custom or creed.

Sachal's ecstasy was the ascent of his heart to the Unseen. Music helped him to ascend and move in a new atmosphere of the Spirit. One day, he fell ill. No medicine cured him. But his heart aspired to the Spirit. All of a sudden, some ladies arrived at Darazan, the spot where Sachal lay ill. They were reputed to be good singers: they had faith in God. They came for Sachal's *darshan*. He looked at them and said to a brother who sat near him, "My physicians have arrived. Blessed be the Name of Allah!

The ladies started singing. They sang in faith: they sang with longing in their hearts. And as they sang, their eyes were touched with tears. Sachal listened to the songs, then got up, and was cured! "Music," Sachal said, "is the healer of illness!"

Music dedicated to the One Name of the Beloved intoxicated him. No other intoxicant, neither *bhang* nor grape wine, did he desire. "The seeker," he said, "should drink cup after cup of Wisdom (*marfat*) from the hands of the Teacher (*murshid*), and in the Teacher's Eye of Compassion behold the Image Divine and be absorbed in it." In a poem Sachal says:

> O cup-bearer!
> I want not grape wine.

> Give me to drink of the wine of Unity
> And be freed of all separation!

It is easy to understand why there was a conflict between Sachal and the *mullahs* (orthodox priests) of Islam. Sachal was a mystic: the *mullah* represented the ecclesiastic class. Sachal aspired to build his life in love. The *mullahs* could not outgrow "creeds". Sachal said, "Creeds I cannot accept. My place is not among the orthodox nor the heretics." Sachal saw the underlying unity of the Hindu and the Muslim. He says in a poem:

> Hindus and Muslims
> Are all emanations
> Of the One Name–Aliph!

All peoples and races have issued out of the One. In this faith of his Heart was the secret of Sachal's life. Sachal regarded national and credal differences as accidents of time. Sachal saw the unity of races and religions in the One Eternal. Realise this, says Sachal, and bloom as bloom the roses of spring. Sachal adds, "Even if, like Mansur, the Iranian mystic, you are crucified, cling to this faith in the One Eternal Love!"

The *mullahs* of Islam rose as one man against Sachal. To them, this great Teacher of Truth boldly said:

> Burn the books to ashes and dust,
> Thus hath the murshid taught me!
> He, too, hath taught me
> To know the Eternal!
> To everyone of you, I say,
> "Thou must first know thyself,
> Then walk the Way of Love!"
> Of this Way of Love
> Hath my Teacher taught me.

The *mullahs* complained against Sachal to the Mir–the ruler of Khairpur. But the *Mullahs* could not prevail against the poet-mystic. The ruler was Sachal's friend and disciple. Sachal realised that the worst enemies of religion were they of its own household. Sachal says in one of his poems, "Not until these temples and mosques, which are the haunts of sectarianism, are renounced, may one hope that man will walk the Way of Truth." In another poem, Sachal sings:

> Behold the justice of love.
> It granteth freedom from all creeds!

As a true Sufi, Sachal had a heart which embraced all men and all religions as manifestations of the One Eternal God. Sachal sings in his poems, of the Devi and the *Guru Granth Sahib*. Rich, indeed, was Sachal's reverence for Guru Nanak. Sachal named his dear disciple Yusuf as "Nanak Yusuf". At Sachal's feet sat Muslim and Hindu disciples, to sing of the One Beloved, adored by seers and *dervishes* of Islam, and the Hindu faith.

Abul Fazl, who too was a Sindhi and who served as a minister in Akbar's cabinet, wrote for a Hindu temple in Kashmir, the following beautiful lines. I quote them as they echo the very essence of Sachal's teaching of the unity of all races and religions.

> O God! In every temple
> I see the worshippers that seek Thee.
> And in every tongue I hear
> Thy servants who sing Thy Name!
> Islam and the Hindu Faith
> Do both feel after Thee!
> Each declares,
> Thou art One!
> And Thou hath no equal!

[3]

A Beautiful story is related of Sachal as a student. Sent to school to receive education, he recited the first letter, "Aliph", and then refused to go further!

"Aliph", the first letter, stands for the "First One". When asked to say "Bey", (the second letter in the alphabet), Sachal said, "Aliph, the First, is Allah–the Eternal. He is the One Only Reality."

Many poems of Sachal sing this thought, again and again, "Is not Aliph, the first letter, enough?" Bey, you say, is the second letter. How can there be a second beside Allah–the First? To speak of "Bey" beside Aliph, the Eternal, would be to deny Him who is the First and Last of life, the Alpha and Omega of existence. A knowledge of outer things is of little avail, Sachal said. Is not Aliph enough? Libraries of books are around men, but they are still so far from the Light! If the heart be dark, books can teach nothing!

Sachal, it is true, studied *"illim"*, external knowledge. He studied Persian and Arabic. But he learnt from *fakirs* and mystics and from Nature and the Heart within, more than he did from books. He absorbed the influences of Nature and the inspirations of the great Sufi singers and poets. And Sachal studied the scripture of the Heart. The one word of the Heart was "Allah", and Allah was to him the Beloved. Sachal studied in the School of Love. The longing to see the Beloved was as a flame in his heart. In the wasted wreckage of human life, he saw still the secret of Love.

What is the highest aim of life? "To live," said Socrates, "devoted to Wisdom."

"Wisdom and Love," Sachal said, "are the dominant aspirations of life." To live thus is to commune with the Holy Spirit. This communion is experienced (1) in visions and

(2) in wakeful hours. Wakeful hours are the hours of simple life. So, be not dominated by desires and worldly goods.

The true man is the man of communion with the Divine Spirit. In such a man is kindled the Light. When, in the Heart within me, is kindled the Light, the Beloved reveals His face. He whose life is communion with the Beloved is the true man. Him we call a *dervish*.

Sachal was a *dervish*. The true *dervish* communes with the Holy Spirit (1) by meditation; (2) by prayer; (3) by contemplation; (4) by *seva* (service) of the poor; (5) by longing and aspiration in dreams and visions; (6) by denial of worldly goods; (7) by music, songs of devotion and heavenly love; (8) by service of the *murshid* – the Teacher – one who refrains from the lusts of the world and has Light in his heart.

Such a man – the true *dervish* is nearer to silence than to speech. To him, the One Reality is the Beloved. One is He, and without Him the world is nought. This world is a veil, of the World Invisible, which, also, is a veil. Behind the veils is the Beloved, ever calling to man, "Be annihilated!"

Millions are the Names of the One. The noblest is Love. The most ancient is Love. The teaching of the sages, prophets and saints, the *guru-upadesh* of all the truly great ones, is Love. The witness of the Holy Spirit in the Heart, in the lives of Krishna and Jesus, of Nanak and Kabir – in the lives of the holy ones of humanity – is Love.

Sachal says, "Learn to love him who says he is your foe!" Does he bring you strife and hate? Give him in return, the love of your heart. Look at yon tree! Stone after stone is flung at it. What does the tree give in return? Fruits or flowers! Does a man hurt you? Give him the healing of your love!

The essence of Religion, Sachal said, is love, not sectarian strife. He asked his disciples not to quarrel about creeds. He said that he offered his loving salutations to all, that in all he beheld the One Beloved. In Rama and in Rahim, he saw the One. Sachal added, "I see the One in Ravana, too! In Krishna and in Kansa, I see the Eternal Love!"

Some Muslims came to Sachal, one day, and said, "A Hindu in a village is become a Muslim. Why won't you rejoice?" Sachal smiled and said, "If, indeed, a *mullah* had become a Muslim, it would have been a matter of joy!"

Sachal's teaching to his disciples was in these few words, "Be transformed! Be new men, by passing through the fire of devotion!"

In Sachal's teaching, the *salik*, the pilgrim on the Path, regards the service of the poor and needy as a mark of true spiritual life. He serves by his money, his tongue and his pen, his teaching, his prayers, his worship, his silent blessings. Sachal repeatedly urged that a true Sufi made others happy. "Give succour to the needy," he taught, not merely by words of mouth but by the noble example of his life. "Give help to the sick and suffering ones. Give comfort to sad hearts. Give consolation to the afflicted."

Sachal Sang: he seldom wrote his songs. And as he stood on his feet to sing, tears streamed from his eyes. And, over and over again, he said:

> See not my sins,
> And see not my wrongs,
> Beloved! Be gracious to me—
> A sinner and a servant at Thy door!

And again:-

> Unclean am I
> And full of stains!
> Open Thou the veil
> And speak to me in Mercy,
> O Merciful One, Al-Rahman!
> That I may see Thy Beauteous face!

Sachal's songs are radiant with the inspiration of the Love of God and Illumination of the Heart. One of the rulers of Sind, the Mir of the Khairpur State, was Sachal's disciple. Sachal asked him to be just and kind to Muslims and Hindus alike. Some of Sachal's earnest appeals to the Ruler remind one of what a Sufi said to Harun al-Rashid, the great Caliph:

> The country is thy house,
> The people are thy progeny.
> If an old woman sleeps at night
> Without having had her meals,
> She would hold thee responsible
> On the Day of Judgement!

In a brief, beautiful line in one of his poems, Sachal tells us he is come into this world to harmonise and reconcile, to bring all men together in one Brotherhood. He reminds us that he is come as an *ashkara*, a "Revealer". He is come to reveal unity and to ask us all to turn away from sectarian strifes to the Path of Love.

Who will walk the Way of Love? He who will be "intoxicated". Yet, it is not grape wine Sachal wants. "Give me," he says, "the wine of unity, the wine of wisdom." He asks for that true intoxication, which is absorption in the One – the Shining One and His Messengers.

Sachal communed with the Love Eternal. So did Mansur. A great Sufi poet of Sind, Bedil speaks of Sachal as "Mansur-like, intoxicated with Love."

Not "opinion", but "Truth" was his watchword. And in his heart was the longing that his life and words would be a voice of *Haq*, of *Sat*, of Eternal Truth. He taught his disciples the truth that to attain *Haq*, they should first be ready to adore Him as the Lord of aspiration and pain. In a poem, he says:

> Innumerable be the books you read. Of what avail are they?
> Many be your meritorious acts. Of what avail are they?
> Far are you from the Beloved, if there be not the longing in your heart!

"Be absorbed each moment," Sachal says, "in the white radiance of the Beloved!" Be absorbed, and you will know that the Master is but one, that in every Picture, the King hath entered Himself. Yes, in every picture – every race and religion, every prophet and saint, every scripture and song – is the Shining One revealed. In the *Qur'an* and the *Gita* is the One, Sachal says; in Isa and Ahmed is the One. Yes, in Ravana and Hanuman is still the One. The Beloved hath entered into every picture – into all!

Many there be who are on the pilgrim path, but how many are on the Path of Love? Move on! Look straight before you! It may be, on your way you will be lost, again and again. But fear not! Move on the Way with a tranquil mind and a quiet heart. And you will reach, at last, the world where you will be a zero and be lost in the Self. And losing yourself, you will find your Self within, in the presence of the Beloved!

Over and over again, Sachal says, "Be not imprisoned in the jail of 'I' and 'me'. He who hath transcended self – he verily hath attained the Highest. He hath become Perfect!" Such a one, Sachal says, "knows no difference between the Hindu and the Muslim. For Allah is the Lord of all and in all shines the One Picture Divine!

Sachal sounds the notes of Unity of Love again and again. He says:

> The One is within thee.
> The One is outside thee!
> Inside thy shirt is One Beloved.
> In thee, in me, in him, in every place
> The One alone doth speak!

The central thought in the message of Sachal to the modern man, I interpret in a few words thus:

> Awake! Awake!
> Awake this very hour today!
> Awaken to the City of Light!
> Be not in love with sin.
> Think no evil of any man.
> Be strong.
> Strive not for greatness, wealth, applause.
> Strive for truth, purity, courage.
> And as a brother among thy brothers be.
> Listen to the lonely song
> Of the poor and forlorn,
> And learn to share with them what you possess,
> And bear witness to the One—the Shining One!

YUSUF, THE BEAUTIFUL

"I have kept my pledge!"

---

[1]

The Beautiful was to him a manifestation of the Divine. He meditated on the Beautiful and his thoughts swept on from flower to star, until he felt he was absorbed in the Eternal.

And he himself was so beautiful. Travelling in Arabia, he had occasion to call on a wealthy merchant. In his house was staying, as a guest, the daughter of an Amir (a rich ruler). She saw Yusuf, and she gazed at his face again and again. She was thrilled with his beauty. And losing self-control, she opened out her heart to him and said, "Yusuf, be mine! I am thine!"

But in Yusuf's heart was a longing for the Eternal. Yusuf's whole soul desired to simplify his life and concentrate it on Eternal Beauty. Yusuf sought his rest in the holy place of his heart, not in marriage with a rich ruler's daughter. So, as he heard the words of the girl, "Yusuf be mine! I am thine!" he trembled from head to foot and he said to himself, "Escape! Escape!" Within him was the resolve to escape the illusion of woman and wealth.

Yusuf was well-versed in books. Like Abelard of France, he could stir multitudes with his eloquence. But I love him not for his learning, but because the idea filled him that life was richer than learning. He longed for a life of purity. He was convinced that the pure in heart would see the Divine Beauty.

As he thought of the words of the daughter of a rich ruler, he grew afraid of her. "I have not," he said to himself, "the riches of the world. She may speak to her father and make my position difficult. I had better leave Arabia altogether. I seek Allah alone!"

Yusuf leaves Arabia for Egypt. Egypt was a land of mystery; in Egypt lived, in those days, a great Muslim *fakir* (yogi) named Junnuna. One of his favourite maxims was: "Truth is the sword of God." Junnuna's words were always tender, compassionate, and full of the love that understands and heals. One could say of him what Sultan Valad said of his father, Jalal'ud-Din Rumi, "All his words are mercies from the Heavenly King."

[2]

To this Teacher of renown, Yusuf goes with a longing in his heart to realise that God is, indeed, closer than hands and feet, and that the soul can truly blend herself with the Beloved in one undivided being.

Yusuf goes to the great Egyptian Teacher to receive initiation. Four long years pass by. Not once does his Teacher ask Yusuf, "Young man! What dost thou want of me?"

Yusuf comes everyday to his Guru's place and listens to what the Teacher tells his group. And every night Yusuf sheds tears of love and longing. "When, O Lord!" he cries out, "shall I receive initiation?"

Four years and more pass by, and Yusuf no longer can repress the longing in his heart. Coming to his Guru and bowing down to him in reverence, Yusuf says, one day, as tears flow down his cheeks, "Master! In the Great Name of God, I beg of you to initiate me."

The Master hears him but says nothing.

One day, he calls Yusuf to himself and says to him, "Open your right hand."

And as Yusuf opens it, the Master place in it a chest and says, "Yusuf! In thy hand I place this closed chest. With this, cross the River Nile, go to the other side. There lives a man who knows me. Thou wilt know him by the name I give thee. Give him this chest, as a I give it to thee – closed!"

Yusuf starts on his journey. The chest in his hands, but what is there in the chest? He is curious to know. And, on the way, his mind tells him, again and again! "Open the chest: see what is in the chest! Then close the chest and, to the man on the other side, give the chest closed."

Yusuf surrenders to the agitation of his mind. He opens the chest, when, lo and behold, out of the chest runs a rat. Yusuf is unable to catch it. Yusuf's heart was filled with sorrow.

"What shall I do?" he asks himself. "Shall I proceed on my journey and meet the man on the other side? Or shall I to my Master return? Alas! I have not obeyed him. I have proved unworthy of the task he entrusted to me."

Yusuf's beautiful eyes shed copious tears of repentance. And, when the heart is contrite and lowly, voices are heard within. Yusuf, hears a voice, "Go onward with the empty chest."

And onward he goes, until he reaches the other side of the river, meets the man and gives him the empty chest. The man is no ordinary man. The man is a rare and lofty soul. The man is a sage. He lives in retreat, far away from multitudes. He spends much time in silence.

And Yusuf asks "Why live you in silence, away from the crowds?

And the sage answers, "I worship Truth, but the crowds are swayed by power, which is held by violence or threat of violence. To Truth, not to power, I give reverence."

And, pausing for a minute, the sage asks, "Whence come you? And why? And what is your name?"

Yusuf says, "I come from Junnuna, my Master in Egypt. Yusuf is my name. My Master sends to you, sire, this chest. But I have more to tell."

Yusuf hands over the chest to the Sage. He opens it. He finds it empty. He smiles and says, "Tell me no more, Yusuf! I understand!"

Then, pausing for a minute, he says, "Yusuf, did you ask Junnuna, your Master in Egypt, in the name of Allah, to give you initiation?"

Yusuf says, "Yes, sire!"

The sage says, "Your Master, in sending you here, has tested you. You have been found wanting. In this chest was a rat. The chest is now empty. You could not take care of a little rat. How may the Master trust you with the Great Mystery, the Secret of the Lord?"

And Yusuf's eyes are touched with tears. He bows in lowly reverence to the Sage and says, "Sire, I have sinned. Forgive me! And intercede for me with my Master to forgive me. I feel ashamed of my conduct! I repent!"

The Sage smiles, and Yusuf could hope again.

[3]

Yusuf is a man with the make-up of a mystic, a saint, but he is, at the time I am thinking of, still in quest of God. He was still a *jignasu* (seeker). He is a lonely soul. He pines for God.

He now returns to Egypt, deeply ashamed. He cannot hold his head up before the Teacher, his Guru. But Yusuf is not become a pessimist, rather has the longing within him grown. And there is a deeper hope in his heart that he will yet achieve the quest.

Junnuna smiles and said, "Yusuf, look up! Didst thou see the Sage?"

Yusuf says, "Master, I saw him and was blessed!"

The Master asks, "And didst thou give him the chest I gave thee?"

Yusuf says, "Master, you know it all. I gave him your chest, but oh, on my way to him, I had to wrestle with my mind. But who, unaided, may overcome his mind? It is a storm. It is a flood. It is a fire. It overwhelms. I opened the chest on the way and the rat ran out. And when I gave the chest to the Sage, he understood it all, and he smiled. And though I had fallen, he blessed me. I come back to you, Master, crest – fallen! I betrayed your trust. I repent! Forgive me!"

The Master said, "Thou hast come to me nearer after the fall, for every fall leads to a rise upward. And at every step is cast the die of Love. His Mercy everywhere doth show itself. And when thou dost see that a brother goeth astray, remember, his going astray, too, is a veil, and beneath the veil He hides. For in every movement is His Will, and in His Will we live and all the worlds. So, be not sad! I did it all to test thee. Thou didst fail in the test, and thou hast repented, and repentance hath quickened thy evolution. In thee is a soul of wondrous beauty, but the beauty has yet to shine. And, I believe, the day is not a far when thy life will become a radiant lantern, wherein God's Light will shine thorugh and through."

Yusuf sheds tears. Yusuf is become new. Day after day, he sits at the Master's feet to learn, to practise and to grow. In him now sings a song the Master alone can fully understand. In him a voice had grown that melts the hearts of men and makes their souls musical and strong. Yusuf now knows that for him to live is to follow the love of the All Beautiful, from life to death and through death into Life for Evermore. Yusuf's self is dead. Yusuf's memories and desires are dead. He finds himself in Him. The Master has blessed Yusuf. He has been found fit to receive initiation "in the Name of Allah, the Compassionate".

[4]

One day, the Master sends for Yusuf and says to him, "My child! My work in thee is accomplished. It is time for thee now to return to Arabia, thy native land. Back to thy people go and teach them how to live and grow."

And Yusuf says, "Master! Infinitely hast thou blessed me. And my gratitude, you know, lives in my heart for ever! In obedience to your wishes I go, back to my people in Arabia. Give me your parting words and your parting benediction."

And the Master says, "Blessings of the All-Good, the All-Beautiful, shine upon thee already. Thou needst no parting words from me, but thou dost ask me, and never in this life and never in the Life for Evermore, can I now say 'no' to thee. Then hear what thou knowest already,

"(1) Exalt me not before men. Nor tell thou anyone of the visions thou hast seen nor of the voices thou hast heard. Speak thou to men as one of them, so that they may judge of what thou wilt teach them on its own merits, and accept it or reject it as they will. Truth is its own evidence to them who truly seek.

"(2) Speak not to men from the books which they read in vanity and vainglory. For all knowledge which is not of the Beloved is a burden and a snare!

"(3) Argue not with any, but speak of Allah and His Servants out of thy heart, my child, that he hath illumined with Light!"

Yusuf bows to the Master and says, "I shall do as ordered. So help me, Allah!"

[5]

Yusuf returns to Arabia. He fain would teach, but where are they who would listen? Many are called, but few are they who understand. Yusuf has a beautiful face. His voice is beautiful. But great Love is silent, and in silence we truly understand. Yet, how few there be who would sit in silence and learn! And how fewer still who have the longing to be united with the Beloved! Men prefer the colours of the picture-house and the scent of roses and the music of halls to the beauty and radiance of a Teacher of Truth and Love! His roses never fade, but men will not come to the Rose-garden of Truth.

Many come to hear Yusuf, at first, but soon the number dwindles. Yusuf meets his little group everyday and feels happy to speak to them. His words are not many, but they are radiant. They go into the hearts of his little group.

The majority of men were under the influence of the *mullahs* (Muslim Preachers). They are dead against Yusuf. What does he teach? He speaks of the Beloved, and the City of Union, and the Face of Beauty that makes every atom articulate, and the Voice of Love coming from near and far, and of souls as pearls in the Sea of Love, and of "Love-lorn nightingales" (the seekers and lovers) singing of the Beautiful One. The *mullahs* lift up their united voice against Yusuf. The Mullahs call him a heretic. Crowds who have no judgement are swayed by the *mullahs'* propaganda against this pure lover of God, this profound Teacher of the Hidden Wisdom. The *mullahs* raise the cry, "This heretic, Yusuf, is an enemy of the *Qur'an* and the Prophet. Yusuf is a vile corrupter of religion. Away with him!"

One day, Yusuf sits at the door of a mosque. A man enters the mosque. His name is Ibrahim. Yusuf sees Ibrahim and asks him, "Brother, won't you give me a verse from the Qur'an?"

Ibrahim looks at Yusuf and says, "Fallen from the Law of Righteousness art thou, O man!"

Indeed, in his journey to the "Rose-Garden of Union," the beloved of God must, again and again, be chastened and chastised in order that he may grow in humility – the secret of saints. As soon as Yusuf hears these words, "Fallen from the Law of Righteousness art thou, O man!" he falls at Ibrahim's feet and sheds tears! After many minutes does Yusuf raise his head and, then, he says in deep humility:

"Ibrahim! Blessed are you among mortals! You have blessed me! From dawn to dusk did I recite the *Qur'an* today, but my mind melted not and I shed not a single tear. But on hearing your words, I have gone into a different state. You tell me that I am fallen from the Law of Righteousness. So many call me 'fallen', fallen from the Law. Now I understand why they call me so. Bless me that I may grow in humility and grace!"

Many spread wrong reports against Yusuf. Many called him names. Yusuf listens to words of censure and praise with unwavering mind. A time comes when the people begin to understand him and call him "a picture of beauty and humility". His life becomes a symbol of the wonder of Divine Love!

One day, there comes to Yusuf a young man named Abdul. He is a disobedient son. He has gone astray. He is a gambler. He has lost his senses.

Yusuf says to him, "As a man calleth another to himself on business, so doth God call the sinners to himself. God hath 'business' with them. God's business is to forgive the sinners and heal them and make them whole." As soon as Abdul hears these words, he begins to dance. He tears his clothes and flings them on the roadside. He runs to a graveyard and falls down unconscious.

Yusuf goes to bed at night with a heavy heart. He is thinking of Abdul, the mad young man. Yusuf has a dream that night. And in the dream he hears the voice of his guardian angel. The voice says to him, "Abdul repents of his sins and you must take care of him."

Yusuf goes to the graveyard and places in his lap the head of the young man and prays for him. Yusuf says he cannot leave Abdul. Yusuf stayes on at the graveyard. After three days, Abdul wakes up from deep slumber. He is no longer mad. He has recovered his senses. Yusuf praises God, "Blessed art Thou, O Lord! Thou dost heal the sick and restore the insane!"

To Yusuf come the sick and distressed. He heals them with his touch and the gaze of his pure, compassionate eyes.

[6]

The *mullahs* still speak ill of Yusuf, but their influence on multitudes has declined. The people have began to understand Yusuf better. Many have learnt to revere him as a holy man, a saint of God. Yet some remain who scoff at him. Yusuf gives glory to God for all the praise men bestow on him and for all the censure poured upon him by the scoffers.

Yusuf goes with a few handsome youths into solitary places and discourses to them on the profound mysteries of spiritual life. The scoffers say that Yusuf is infatuated with the youths and spread scandals against him. Yusuf has respect for women. Some of them, full of tender grace and beauty, are devoted to him. Once again, the scoffers spread scandals against Yusuf.

Yusuf gives his love to all. He fain would draw sinners to God. He mingles with drunkards and the *mullahs* invent stories against him. But Yusuf knows that not a leaf stirs without the Will of God. And he bows to scandal-mongers. They, too, enter into the Plan of God to work out His Will. Yusuf is at peace with all.

[7]

In Arabia, there is a town named Nishapur. A merchant of this place has a very beautiful wife. The merchant had to leave town for some days to recover money from a debtor. But the merchant must first arrange for the board and lodge of his wife. She is so beautiful. He must not leave her in her lonely house. He can only leave her in the house of a pure, trustworthy man.

He remembers there is one such man in Nishapur. They call him Abu Usman. He is a *tapasvi*, a man of self-control. The merchant's wife comes and lives in Abu Usman's house. One day, Usman sees her beautiful face and is bewitched. Usman's mind is agitated. He goes to a religious teacher, Hafiz, and opening out his heart, says, to him "Save me, in Allah's Name!" Hafiz sends him to Yusuf.

Usman moves out to meet Yusuf. He lives in a far-off town. There, Usman falls into the hands of some of the detractors of Yusuf. They say to Usman, "You are so good. Your life is pure. You are a fakir, a *tapasvi*. Strange that you wish to go to Yusuf! He is not pure and he mingles with the drunkards. Meet him not! If you go to his house, your reputation will suffer. Return!"

On hearing this, Usman returns to Nishapur. He is afraid of what people would say if he went to meet Yusuf.

And Hafiz sends Usman back to Yusuf.

Usman hears again wild reports against Yusuf. Usman is firm. He finds out Yusuf's house. What does he see? In the house, near the door, sits a man, well-advanced in age. His face is beautiful. His eyes are radiant, his words are sweet. Usman says, "Here is a king amongst men!"

Usman salutes Yusuf. Yusuf salutes Usman in return, and says to him, "Welcome, brother! Sit down!"

Then Yusuf talks to him of spiritual life, of the treasures of Wisdom, of the vision of His Face that illumes the day, of the peerless King, who is exalted above description and explanation, of the beauty of the Beloved, whose vision emancipates the heart, of the Light of Love that calleth all heavenwards.

Usman is thrilled. Usman looks, again and again, into Yusuf's bewitching eyes, and Usman looks around. Usman finds that near Yusuf is a bottle and a cup. Usman is surprised. He says to Yusuf, "Your face is so beautiful. Your eyes are lit up with light. Your tongue is sweet as the song of a nightingale. Your talk is captivating. But why have you kept near you this wine bottle and a cup?"

Yusuf said, "Listen, brother! I live in holy poverty. I have no money to buy a vessel for water. So, I have cleansed this bottle and filled it with pure water, and if a thirsty man or woman cometh, I offer him or her water in this cup!"

Usman is, amazed. He says, "O, the sinners! They talk ill of you. Why do you let them censure you? Why don't you behave differently?"

Yusuf says "Usman! I behave as I do that scoffers may censure me! When I become notorious as a bad character, no one will leave his beautiful wife in my house. So shall I be freed from temptation. And my soul shall rejoice in Allah alone!"

Usman understands that in Yusuf's words there is a reference to him. Usman falls down at the feet of Yusuf and says, "You are the Moses of our day. You are a singer of Allah! And in your songs is a wealth of the wonder of the Beloved and His Divine Love. Accept me as a disciple!"

[8]

The Beauty of the Beloved absorbed Yusuf. And he kept awake at night, until, gazing and gazing at the beauty of the silver stars, he would enter into the presence of the Beloved. And often he stood on the floor, in supreme devotion to the Divine King. To Yusuf, the world and its wonders were the shadows which would pass away, but the Beloved would still abide. His voice—the voice of Love—he heard in men and women, in the beasts of the jungle and the birds of the air, in saints and angels, in sinners and the fallen, in children and the broken ones, in mountains and rivers, in seas and the swinging of the stars.

In the hour of death, Yusuf gave loving greetings to all and said, "Beloved! I have kept my pledge. I have done my task. I have sounded Thy Trumpet for love of Thee, to draw men and women to Thy Love. And now I come to Thee! Forgive my trespasses, Beloved, and accept me! I come to Thee!"

[9]

Here are a few more of his "Sayings":

He who knows that God seeth every act, he will tremble to do evil!

*

He who concentrates on the Beloved forgets all.

*

He who is absorbed in the Beloved is censured and persecuted by the world. But, in return, he giveth the world compassion and love!

*

He who has true love for the Beloved is simple, unostentatious. He loves but keeps afar from publicity!

*

As a man dives, deeper and deeper, into the Beloved, the longing in him grows, to be annihilated in Love.

*

In the Qur'an a we read, "He loveth them that love Him!" The Beloved's love made Yusuf's body lean and his eyes radiant, and his heart a mansion of Light. Centuries have passed since Yusuf passed away, but his name is a Star of Light, which shineth for ever!

PARASI: A MUSLIM YOGI
"To walk the Will of God is religion!"

[1]

Come with me, in imagination, to a country beyond the bounds of India. The country is called Parasa. It is near Iraq, in Turkestan. The inhabitants of Parasa are Muslims.

In an Islamic family in Parasa was born a child. His parents were poor and he received little education. But the grace of God was upon him. He grew in years and aspiration. He got illumination. Is not illumination better than all the education of the universities of the world?

This child of grace and beauty, born centuries ago, grew to be a *bhakta* of the Lord and a teacher of men and angels. He came to be named after his birth-place. He was named Parasi–"belonging to Parasa".

He lived in a cottage, but there was, in his heart, a longing for the Eternal. His heart was not in the things of the earth. As a youth, he dreamed of the True, the Good, the Beautiful. He had no dreams of money or power. Away from the "madding crowds", he lived his life apart from the world. And again and again, he put himself the ancient question, "What is life? And why is man born on the earth?"

Gradually, the thought grew on him that there was no growth without obedience to a law. Then grew on him the thought that to grow in the Life Beautiful, he must renounce earthly desires. Passion made a man ugly, deformed. Purity was the secret of beauty and radiance.

One day, a strange, mystic impulse stirs him. He leaves his cottage. His Home is elsewhere. He goes to a forest. He stays there for some years. His soul ripenes. He learns to meditate. He teaches himself self-control. And he makes the supreme discovery that the world and its pleasures pass away; the Eternal alone is.

Again and again, you may find him speaking to himself, telling his body, "I will not let you have what you clamour for!" The body clamours for comfort, the body would fain keep away from work and toil, and would like to be lazy or indulge in luxury. So, this great *bhakta* teaches his body to be moderate in eating and sleep. Eating much and sleeping much are sins against the spiritual law of the moderation. A few morsels of food are enough for him. One day, he is tempted to eat one more morsel. Then, he repents, sheds tears. He tells his body, "Break not the divine rule of moderation, if thou wilt grow in health and radiance." And he teaches his body, also, to be simple in dress. For some days, he wears leaves of trees and feel happy!

So, in the forest he lives, in silence and in fellowship with the birds and the animals, with trees and the flowers, with the stars and the running brook. He grows in fellowship with nature. He learns simplicity, the secret of the radiant life. He learns meditation, the secret of the saints. His face grows in beauty. His heart grows in sympathy and the power of understanding. He sings, he dances, he weeps he cries again and again, "Be Thou not afar, my Lord! But keep me at Thy feet always!"

He becomes a Yogi. He sees the Light and hears Voices within him. And, one day, a Voice says to him, "Finished are thy labours, my child! Return to thy native place and open there a School of spiritual wisdom. For unhappy are men and they long for a message of hope and healing!"

He listens to his inner Voice. It leads better than all the books and all the arguments of learned men. He opens in his native place a spiritual School. Many join it. He comes each day and, in his simple way, teaches the profound truths of life.

One day, a member of the School comes to him and says, "Master! I have a longing to feed you. Won't you come to my house? It will be blessed by your presence."

The next day, he goes there. He was a Muslim, but he eats no flesh. Yet, he does not compel members of his School to give up eating flesh. He believes that life teaches better than lips, and a servant of God must impose nothing on others, only bear witness to the truth and beauty of the higher life.

The yogi now sits down to meals. He hardly puts the first morsel in his mouth when he finds that it was a piece of flesh. He immediately takes it out and exclaims, "Blessed be the Lord!" He washes his mouth, quietly gets up and says to his host, "Brother! You have been kind. You have prepared for me food in love. I accept it. You did not know, brother, that I take no flesh. But you have given me love in abundance. Blessed be the Lord!"

Then he talks to his host of spiritual life and the way to Wisdom. The host has no food to offer to the yogi. But his talk hath lent new beauty to the meeting, his talk hath opened to the host a treasure of man's divine heritage. He is a new man! And the yogi returns home, repeating the *mantra*, "Blessed be the Lord!"

This one truth he teaches, again and again, and he teaches it with power, because he lives it in his daily life. "Let not your hearts be troubled," he says, "but in all stations of life, say, 'Blessed be the Lord!' If your bodies be sick or in pain, say, 'Blessed be the Lord!' For, nothing happens without the Will of Allah. Not a leaf stirs, not a hand moves, not an eye winks, not a tongue tells, not an ear hears, without the Will of Allah. To walk the Will of Allah is religion."

Is it a wonder that such a man wins quiet sovereignty over multitudes? His name travels to Turkestan. And the beauty of his simple, quiet life inspires and enthralls the Muslims of Iraq.

[2]

There comes to him, one day, a man, his face lit up with a strange light. "Whence are you?" asks the yogi.

And the man says, "Master! I come from Egypt. Your hallowed name has travelled to that far-off place. I come to have your blessings. And may I say one thing which is in my heart, Master?"

"Speak without reserve," says the Yogi.

And the man says, "In Egypt, Master, dwells a Beloved of the Lord. He is greater than my weak words may tell. He spends much of his time in silence. And we go to him and sit at his feet in silence. We sit and are filled with a strange power. It has changed the life of multitudes. There is an end of crime in the city where dwells this Seer of Silence. Dishonesty hides its head. Purity prevails. Master! I come not only to have your blessings but to entreat you to go and see him. He would rejoice to see you. We regard him as greater than a hundred Pharaohs of our ancient Land. For, this Beloved of God, this Seer, this Mystic of Silence, is a lover and he worships beauty and truth. And in his presence, all things, all words, all ideas – story and song and music – are clothed in the radiance of the Spirit. In a hundred cities and villages of Egypt, thousands, young and old, are absorbed in this Man, who is absorbed in silence, and are being moulded into wisdom by his gentle, beautiful life."

The Yogi's heart is filled. He says, "Blessed art thou, brother! Thou hast spoken to me of the Beloved of God. Tomorrow, I go!"

And the Yogi tells the members of his School, "I go on a pilgrimage to Egypt, tomorrow!" Some tell him that Egypt is far-off. But the Yogi says, "In Egypt dwells the Beloved of God, and if I had to cross seven seas to see him, I still would go!"

The next day, he wears the pilgrim's white, simple clothes, and starts on his pilgrimage.

The Yogi reaches Egypt. He arrives at the house of the Beloved of God. He is advanced in age: his hair is white as snow. His eyes are closed. The Yogi bows down in reverence to the Beloved, and says, "Bless me. I ask it in the Name of Allah!"

It is a rule of the life of the Beloved that he never turns away anyone who asks of him anything in the Name of Allah. The Beloved is in meditation. How does he receive the Yogi's vibrations? The Beloved opens his eyes and sees the Yogi. The two gaze each into other's face. The Yogi beholds the beauty of his eyes. How they shine! Old, very old, is he, but his eyes shine with a Light such as never shone in a youth's eyes.

The Beloved opens his lips to speak. He greets the Yogi, "Welcome, O Parasi Yogi! Thrice welcome here. For thy coming have I looked these long weeks and months!"

How does the Beloved know the Yogi and his name? The Yogi knows, and within his heart he says, "Have Egypt and Iraq and the far-off countries of Turkestan produced a single hero worthy to touch the Beloved's shoes?"

And the Yogi bows down before the Beloved in lowly reverence and says, "Master! I have seen you and been blessed. In my heart have I made you my *murshid* (Master). Accept me in the service of your lotus feet and teach me!"

The Beloved looks up, and gazing at the Yogi's radiant face, says, "My child! Man's days are like grass. As a flower of the field he springs and as a flower he fades. For, the wind of Fate passeth over him and he is gone! Thou art, my child, advanced. Thou needst stay here a week—no more! I give thee blessings of my perpetual presence. I enter into thee. I in thee and thou in me! After a week, return to thy place and re-open there the School of Wisdom, for sorrow covereth the hearts of men. They walk through the valley of the shadow of death, and they are so soon to die. Go and comfort them. Go and teach them the Ancient Way that as many as accept it may dwell in the house of the Lord for ever! I have nought else to teach!"

And when the week is over, the Beloved renews his blessings on the Yogi. He goes back home to be a Teacher and a Healer. And on the way he says, again and again, in his heart, "Nothing abides. The earth and the suns and the stars, all shall go – are going, minute by minute – to the Eternal Drift, until no man may know and name them. The Beloved hath lifted me to joy and peace. I go to give, under his blessings, love and joy to some of those who dwell, alas, in the dark house of desire and death!"

[3]

The Yogi returns to his country and re-opens his School of Wisdom. He teaches profound truths in the simplicity and strength of a seer. He shows how men walk the way of desire and soon are dead. He shows how, through the ages of history, men and women in East and West, have eaten and struggled and run the race through hot desires, then slept and vanished quickly, as vanishes the spring that shines upon the day. And he shows that there is a way which man may follow and in this mortal body attain the Immortal. Many come to his School, from far and near. It opens to many, the door of the New Life.

One evening, when his talk with the class was over, a man comes and sits at the Yogi's feet. The Yogi asks, "Whence are you?"

And the man says, "Sir! I come from a far-off place. Your name has travelled far and wide. I heard of you and your holy teaching, and I am come to have your blessings."

The Yogi says to him, "Brother! Speak what you will. Speak without reserve!"

The man says, "Sir! I come from a great distance. I arrived here this morn. I am a stranger here, I need food. I have no friend, no relative here. If you will kindly let me stay in your School and give me daily food!"

The Yogi says, "Brother! I gladly give you leave to stay here."

A few days pass. The Yogi calls the man to his room and says, "Brother! You come every day, but why do you wear black clothes?"

The man says, "Master! If a relative or friend dies, we wear black. It is the custom of our country."

The Yogi asks, "Which of your friends or relatives have you lost?"

The man says, "Master! Five friends. Long did they stay with me. All the five died!"

The Yogi says, "Five friends! So many! And they all died the same day. May I know their names?"

The man says, "Master! I dare not say no to you. You ask and I must tell you. The names of my five friends were Passion, Anger, Greed, Attachment and Egoism. All the five died the same day. All the five were my friends and had stayed with me long. Therefore, I wear black!"

The Yogi calls a servant and says to him, "Turn this man out of the door!"

The man is confounded and says, "Master, have mercy! Do not turn me out of the door! I have not had my noon-meals yet!"

But the Yogi is adamant. He tells the servant, "Turn him out of the door!"

The man says, "I go out of the Hall, but I will cling to the outskirts of this holy house. And I shall hope that, some day, the Master will look upon me with mercy. I know not, but I must have done some wrong!"

And the man sits outside. But his eyes are bright with a strange, mystic light!

At twelve o'clock noon, the Yogi tells the servant, "Call the man in!"

The man is brought before the Yogi, who says, "It is noon – the hour when resident members of the School sit to meals. You are hungry. Have your meals!"

The man feels happy. But as soon as he finished his meals, the Yogi calls his servant again and says, "Turn this man out!"

So is this man turned out seventeen times! And every time the Yogi looks into his face, and every time the Yogi finds that the man's eyes sparkle with a strange, mystic light. Every time the man is seen smiling. His face is calm and quiet.

The Yogi calls the man again and says, "Blessed are you among mortals! I was testing you. I never meant to insult you. But it looked like my insulting you. And I did so seventeen times. And every time you smiled and a spiritual light illumined your eyes. Blessed are you! Your five friends are really dead. You have conquered desires. You have won. Stay with me and bless me every day. Your eyes behold the Secret of Life. Your heart has a vision of the Secret of Wisdom. Feel no longer lonely. Look to me for fellowship and affection. Stay with me, brother! And purify the School with your presence. You will heal many hearts! And in wisdom and love, you will help many of those who stumble, alas, through the dark forest of this life!"

Soon after this, Parasi, the Muslim Yogi, passed to *Brahma-Nirvana*, the Peace of the Eternal!

HATIM HASHIM

*"Not what you choose, but what
He does is the best for you!"*

I see history not as a scene of political struggles and bloodshed, but as the effort of man to understand and discipline, and remake himself. Tolstoy defined history as the life of the nations. History, it is true, is the drama of the nations, but the makers of this drama are not Alexanders and Caesers, Napoleons and Hitlers, Stalins and Churchills. The drama of a nation is the story of its exceptional men – and women – dreaming of life sublime and living it, singing of noble ideals, making music out of languge, and out of music, moulding men into instruments of the Eternal Will.

To this class of "exceptional men" belong saints and sages, seers and singers, and they are the monopoly of no one nation, religion or race. The 'exceptional men' have appeared among all races and religions – among Hindus no less than among Muslims. There is no conflict between Hindu saints and Muslim mystics. The more I study their lives and teachings, the more I grow in the joy of fellowship with them all, realising that there is a wonderful unity between Hindu sages and Muslim *dervishes* of God.

One of these *dervishes* was Hatim Hashim. His life and words have deeply impressed me. Hatim's was a simple life – uneventful, you will say, but it has thrilled me. His words are simple and radiant with the light of a seer and servant of God.

He loved Truth, he worshipped Truth, he lived each day in Truth and Love. He lived a life of *tapasya*. He controlled his appetites. He disciplined his mind and purified his heart. He endured, he suffered, and he waxed in wisdom. A Muslim saint bore witness to Hatim Hashim in pregnant words, "A *mahatma* like Hatim Hashim is a rare jewel in this world."

He received little education. He read little, he wrote little. He spoke from realisation, and out of his mouth came precious pearls of wisdom. This "illiterate" *dervish* was an illuminated one.

He lived in Khorasan. He married a lady who was, like him, devoted to God. "He will provide," she said. She did not let her mind be disturbed by poverty. She cast her cares on the Lord, and the Lord took care of her and Hatim, as He has always taken care of His *bhaktas* and devotees in all countries and all ages.

They came to him from far and near, saying, "Master, teach us!" And he taught profound truths in simple words. The number of his disciples grew from more to more. Speaking to them, one day, he said, "Fellow servants of God! You now are many. I am an illiterate. How long can I teach you? It will be kind of you to help me in choosing someone who may teach you and teach me!"

At a meeting of aspirants, they discussed the question, "Who is a true spiritual leader?"

One of his disciples said, "A warrior of the Lord."

"No," said Hatim Hashim, when they asked him his opinion. "A warrior is a *ghazi*, one who fights and kills others on the battlefied, but a spiritual leader is one who fights himself and becomes a martyr."

Another disciple said, "A spiritual leader is a philanthropist."

"No," said Hatim. "Such a man is a liberal giver, but a spiritual leader must be a receiver of God's grace."

"And who receives the grace of God?" they asked him.

And he answered, "He who looks up to God in the daily trials of life, and whose one only hope is God, and none but God!".

A wealthy man offered Hatim a portion of his wealth. Hatim said, "I will not take from you. I shall take only from the Lord!"

An atheist entered into discussion with him, "Whence have you your daily food?" asked the atheist.

And the *dervish* answered, "From the Store of God!"

The atheist said, "How strange! You receive from the people and you give credit to God!"

And Hatim said, "Have I ever taken aught from you?"

"True," replied the atheist, "you have never taken anything from me. But do you mean to say your daily food descends from Heaven?"

"Not mine alone, but everybody's food cometh from Heaven!"

"Then sit with your doors closed," the atheist said, "and see how food comes to you!"

"You are right," replied Hatim. "I was a child, for two years I sat in my room. Then, too, food came to me–to my very mouth!"

"How can food come to you from Heaven?" the atheist asked.

"As it comes to the bird."

"But what about one who is on the earth?"

"As it comes to the ant!"

The atheist was silenced. And in stillness, tears touched his eyes. Were they the tears of repentance? Humbled and repentant, the atheist asked Hatim for a few words of *upadesh* (instruction). And the holy man said, "Brother, build not thy hope in men! Whatever thou doest, do it as an offering to God!"

What a noble teaching! Does not Sri Krishna say to Arjuna in the *Gita*, "Arjuna! Whatever thou eatest, whatever thou givest in charity, whatever thou drinkest, whatever thou doest, do it as an offering to the Lord."?

On one occasion, Hatim said, "Early in the dawn, Satan comes to me and asks, 'What will you eat?' And I say to him, 'The dead!' Satan asks, 'What will you wear?' And I say to Satan, 'The clothes of the dead!' And Satan asks, 'Where will you dwell?' And I say, 'In the grave!' And Satan finds he had nothing further to say. He leaves me and departs."

It is true, he who wants nothing, he who asks not for good food or good clothes, a good house, he who is dead to this world and is happy to live in the tomb of silence — he cannot be tempted by Satan.

One day, Hatim asked a seeker, "How are you?"

The seeker said, "Happy and peace-filled!"

Then said Hatim, "Brother! Happy is he who has crossed the world's illusions and reached the Shore. Peace-filled is he who has the joy of the spiritual world!"

A man asked Hatim, "What is your deepest desire?"

And Hatim said, "To live in joy, day and night! The day I do not sin in thought or word of deed — against God — is the day of joy for me!"

One day, a man came and said to Hatim, "This man has untold treasure!"

Hatim said, "Yes, he has earned untold treasure. Has he, also, earned endless life? If not, of what use will his wealth be to him in the hour of death?"

In his travels, Hatim reached Baghdad, the seat of the Khalifa. On hearing of Hatim's arrival, the Khalifa sent his men to request Hatim to come to the Khalifa's *darbar*. On arriving at the *darbar*, Hatim said to the Khalifa, "O man of renunciation! *Salaam!*"

The Khalifa is surprised and says, "How am I a man of renunciation? Am I not a ruler of the realm? Renunciation is yours, O *dervish!*"

"No," says Hatim, "you are a man of renunciation."

"How?" asks the Khalifa.

And Hatim answer, "God says, 'The world's wealth is naught.' You have renounced spiritual treasures and collected the world's wealth – nothing! You have renounced the true wealth – of the Spirit. I have but given up the world's wealth and the world's desires, and am intent on spiritual treasures."

Hatim did not know the learning of books, nor the way of scholars. But scholars came to him to learn of him and books may be written to interpret the meaning of his thought-filled words. Wherever he went, he blessed multitudes, and whenever he taught, he illumined and inspired. A whole school of wisdom was in his heart.

He taught all to beware of pride and greed. He referred to three kinds of pride: (1) the pride of the ruler, (2) the pride of the rich, (3) and the pride of the scholar. The third pride, he said, was more fearful than the first or the second.

He spoke of four kinds of "mind": (1) *murda*, (2) *rogee*, (3) *alasi*, and (4) *roshan*. The *murda* mind is the mind of him who is an atheist–denying and defying God. The *rogee* or diseased mind is the mind of the sinner. The *alasi* or lazy mind is the mind of the greedy and selfish man. The *roshan* or illumined mind is of him who, by self-discipline and meditation, lives in the Divine Presence, every day.

As an aid to the devout life, he suggested that the seeker should remember that whatever he does is being seen by God and whatever he says is being heard by God. And in the hour of silence, he said, the seeker should meditate on God as the All Seer.

Hatim emphasised three disciplines for the growth of spiritual life. (1) Whatever you eat or drink or enjoy, remember that God is looking at you. (2) Whatever you say, see that you do not utter a single word of untruth. (3) Whenever you open your eyes to see, take care that your eyes are clean, pure, and not wayward or sold to Satan.

Hatim taught that the seeker after God must practise self-examination every day. And in self-examination, the seeker must ask himself these four questions: (1) In doing service, have I a motive of my own? (2) In speaking anything, am I selfish? (3) In giving alms, do I seek anything for myself in return? (4) In earning or collecting money, do I flatter any or do I stand up in courage and hold money as a trust for the service of others?

Hatim spoke of three stages in the progress of *vairagya* or renunciation. (1) In the first stage, the seeker's strength is faith in God. (2) In the second stage, the seeker learns to suffer, more and more, to glorify God. (3) And in the third stage, the seeker has grown in God's love and, in love, has learnt to forget himself, his all, in God, the Beloved.

Speaking to some of his disciples, one day, Hatim said, "If you will become instruments of the Divine Will, vessels of His grace, choose nothing, but rejoice in the station or the work allotted to you by God. For, remember this, not what you choose, but what He does, is the best for you!"

Hatim's words were simple. His thought was freed from the heavy chains of logic. His simple, aspiring life liberated his mind for concentration. His heart, emancipated from the chaos of desires, rose in silence, in spiritual stillness, to a stage where you see nothing but God, hear nothing but God, and feel nothing but God. It is the stage which statesmen and political leaders understand not, for they see not the emptiness of the things and honours of the earth. It is the stage which is above the reach, of those who seek the bubble of greatness. It is the stage which they reach, who, rising beyond debate and doubt, become children of the Spirit, seeking a way out of the agony, the tears and tragedy of this life, into utter selflessness – into the service of love.

One of these "children of the Spirit" was this holy man of Islam, Hatim Hashim.

AHMED: A LOVER OF ALLAH

"How can I waste any time in Sleep!"

[1]

It was no easy task Muhammad undertook. He believed in his mission. His people scoffed at him. Seeing him, many would cry, "Here cometh the son of Abdullah with his news from heaven!" Many called him "mad". Some said he was a "poet" under the influence of a "*jin*". Some doubted his sanity and proposed to send him a doctor to cure him! Some threw filth at him, and the entrance to his house was often strewn with thorns!

His people, the Arabs, were interested more in blood-feuds, love and wine, than in God, prayer and religion. The Arab poets of his day sang, "Let us enjoy the present day: for soon death will overtake us!"

Here are the words of Arafa, an old Arabic poet, who sang of wine and women, and made fun of God,

> In the morn, at thy coming, I will hand thee a goblet brimming with wine.
> It matters not if thou has drunk already. With me thou wilt drink again!
> And thou wilt drink with my comrades who are youths with faces which shine as the stars.
> Each evening a singing-girl, wearing a striped robe and a tunic of saffron, graces our company.

> Her vestment is open at the neck and amorous hands fondle her!
> My life is surrendered to wine and pleasures.
> I have sold my possessions. I am spending the wealth I gained and all my patrimony.
> Dost thou blame me, O Censor? But say, canst thou make me immortal? Canst thou ward off the fatal moment of death? Then suffer me to lavish my all in enjoyment before Death hath me in his clutches.
> The man of generous impulses drinks deeply while he liveth.
> Tomorrow, O Censor! When thou and I are dead, we shall see which of us twain chose the better part!

To transform such people into a new nation came Muhammad. "O thou, who art covered! Rise up and warn! And thy Lord magnify!" Voices came to him – voices and visions, "I am He! Listen to Me! You are the chosen one! Proclaim the Name of the Lord!" In the month of fasting and penance – the month of *Ramzan* – and in the night of el Kadr, when God's miracles happen and they who receive His mercy become sages or saints – the Voice spoke to Muhammad, "*Iqra*! Recite! Read!" And in fiery letters, he read and recited the following, in a vision spread out before his eyes.

> In the Name of the merciful and compassionate God,
> Read—in the Name of thy Lord!

To this vision, he remained steadfast. The people did not, at first, believe their Prophet. They ill-treated him. They opposed and persecuted him. But he who had been kissed and blessed by Gabriel, God's archangel, believed in the Voice which spoke to him, "Thou art the messenger of God, Muhammad!" And while priests and merchants and chiefs of many tribes stood against him, he stood up as a Prophet, announcing his vision from place to place, inflaming the hearts of those that heard him with the message:

> He is God alone.
> God, the Eternal!

The message conquered, at last, the people of Arabia. The message spread with extraordinary rapidity to many lands. One hundred years after the Prophet had passed on, his message had penetrated into Africa and other parts of Asia.

The life and vision of this illuminated son of the Desert, this consecrated camel-driver who, on Mt. Hira, received from God the command to preach to all the truth, the eternal truth, moved the nations, and his memory thrilled his followers to the end of the their lives. The Khalifas spread Islam to Asia and North-Western Europe. And under the influence of Islam were shaped the lives of not a few Muslims who, in aspiration, illumination and dedication to the Divine, attained the holy heights of some of the great seers of ancient Greece and some of the mighty *rishis* of Aryavarta.

One of these Muslim mystics was Ahmed.

[2]

Ahmed was born at Nishapur. Some of his thoughts remind one of Plato, and like Plato, he was handsome and vigorous. But he was not, like Plato brought up in comfort: nor did he like Plato travel to many lands and absorb the wisdom of those lands. Ahmed drank in deeply of the wisdom of God. In Ahmed's thought, there is the beauty of simplicity. Plato's thought is deep as the sea. In Plato, you find psychology and pedagogy, politics and eugenics, modern metaphysics and Freudian psycho-analysis. Ahmed was a man of meditation rather than of metaphysics. He did the *jap* of "Allah, the Eternal", "Allah, the Great Mystery", "*Subhan Allah!*".

In Ahmed's thoughts, as in the simple story of his life, is the beauty of a mystic who lived in God! Like Meister Eckhart, Ahmed realised that God was the *truth* of life, and that the secret of spiritual life was known to him who refused to let any creature or any earthly thing stand as a barier between him and God. A friend wrote to him a letter and complained of lack of news from Ahmed. He was at his prayers, one day, and the memory of the letter flashed upon him. Then came to him the thought, "This letter-writing stands in the way of Union with God!" So he wrote to his friend, "Kindly do not write to me in future, for I do not wish to write letters and forget God! I desire that you, too, should be absorbed in singing the Name of God. *Salaam!*"

Ahmed was a God-absorbed mystic!

[3]

Ahmed's mother brings him food, one day, and say, "Ahmed! Here is fine food for you, eat it!"

And Ahmed says, "Mother! You are always so good! But I have no craving for fine foods. I wish to eat only what is prepared purely and bought with pure money. The other day, mother, you brought me fine food from a neighbour's house. I learnt that the food was bought with impure money!"

Ahmed believed in the Aryan maxim: As is *anna*, so is *mana*! As is the food, so is the mind!

Ahmed had the refined spirit of a *rishi*. In Nietzsche's conception of the superman, masculine decisiveness is blended with courage. In the Aryan conception of the *rishi*, purity is blended with communion with the Divine. Ahmed had the two great the qualities of the *rishi*. Ahmed was a thinker and a worshipper. His soul was humble and he had not the dictatorial egoism of an aristocrat.

Genius is not hereditary, and Ahmed had a son who inherited none of the great qualities of his father. Ahmed was humble and original. His son was corrupt, a child of luxury and decadence. Ahmed was intuitive, like Wagner's "Parsifal", a "pure fool", the "fool in Allah". Such "fools" redeem the world. Ahmed's son was argumentative, crudely controversial, egoistic.

One day, a well-known devotee of Ahmed comes to see him. Ahmed's son is in his revelry and song. He sees the devotee but had not the courtesy to speak a single word of welcome to him. The devotee meets Ahmed with love and reverence.

And Ahmed says, "Did my son meet you?"

The devotee says, "Master! He saw me and I saw him."

Ahmed understand, then smiles and says, "One night, a neighbour sent us sweets. My wife and I ate them. Then, we learnt that the sweets came from the palace of the king. That night, this boy entered into his mother's womb. There was *rajo-guna* in the king's sweets we ate. In *rajo-guna* was the boy born. He has thus been a *rajo-guni* since his birth. May Allah forgive us!"

[4]

Some disciples said to him, "Master! Tell us about a true devotee of the Lord!"

"Then, listen," he said. "Bahram was my neighbour. He became my friend. He was a wealthy merchant, his caravans carried, for sale in foreign lands, goods worth lakhs of rupees, every year.

"One day, his caravans were looted by robbers on the way. Bahram suffered loss to the tune of several lakhs. I went to console him. I arrived as the sun was setting. Famine was in the land. Bahram thought I, like others, was in the hope of dining. Bahram asked a servant to bring meals for me.

"I said to him, 'Brother! Don't trouble. I came not in the hope of having meals, but to sympathise with you in your great loss!'

"And Bahram said, 'Yes, it is ture I have lost lakhs. But I feel grateful to God. The robbers looted my goods. Thank God, I have looted none! The robbers have robbed a portion of my perishable wealth, but they have not touched the treasure imperishable—the Treasure of faith in Allah, the Compassionate. It is the true Treasure of life!'"

After relating this, Ahmed turned to his disciples and said, "This Bahram is a true devotee of the Lord!"

[5]

Night after night, Ahmed kept awake, singing, "Allah, the Compassionate!" And when a disciple told him once, "Master! Do sleep tonight at least", Ahmed smiled and said, "How can he waste his time in sleep who sees that the Fire of Hades is burning below and the Kingdom of Heaven is calling him above!"

Ahmed kept awake at night to listen to the Call of the Kingdom of Heaven.

The Kingdom called him. The Gleam of Allah, the Eternal, moving to melody, floated before him, until it touched the City of Union. And, one night, he quietly passed into the Light of the Adored and Beloved One.